JUMP FOR JOY

Jump for Joy

HENRY TYLER

KINGSWAY PUBLICATIONS

EASTBOURNE

Front cover photo: The Photo Source

Printed in Great Britain for
KINGSWAY PUBLICATIONS LTD
Lottbridge Drove, Eastbourne, E. Sussex BN23 6NT by
Cox & Wyman Ltd, Reading.
Typeset by CST, Eastbourne, East Sussex.

Contents

Dedicated with love to the members of the body of Christ in Clarendon Church, Brighton and Hove; The Living Word Fellowship, Bombay; Guernsey Christian Fellowship, Channel Islands.

'How can we thank God enough for you in return for all the joy we have in the presence of our God because of you?' (1 Thess 3:9, NIV).

Foreword

Some might argue that the world situation is too serious, too demanding for us to consider a book about joy. The days are evil; we must make the most of the time! Can we afford to be thinking about such trivial distractions? There is a job to be done demanding all our concentration and effort!

Whereas this might sound good sense, it shows a lamentable misunderstanding of the great place of joy in God's provision for his people. Focusing on joy in treacherous days is not to be compared with fiddling while Rome burns. Nor is it to be seen as simply the cream on the cake—a delightful but unnecessary addition to something already perfectly nourishing in its own right.

The apostle Paul argued very differently. It is *because* the days are evil that he instructs the church to make the most of the time by being filled with the Spirit, speaking to themselves in psalms and hymns and spiritual songs, singing and making melody with their heart to the Lord (Eph 5:16–19). God's answer to the lost and guilty world on the day of Pentecost was to unleash on it a company of men who at first sight appeared to be a party of drunks!

They were full of the Holy Spirit and joy, and the joy of the Lord was their strength.

Nehemiah was the first to disclose this secret. In his day, the people experienced constant hostility, many frustrations, daily drudgery and even their own sense of failure, but Nehemiah put first things first. 'Do not be grieved,' he commanded, 'for the joy of the Lord is your strength.'

Some book titles provide no challenge to their author. A book about recent archaeological discoveries in the Middle East does not raise the question, 'But does the author live in the good of it?' To write a book about joy requires a person unembarrassed by his chosen title. Henry Tyler is such a man! His joy is legendary! People known personally to me from Mexico and India immediately smile at the mention of his name. They have shared his joy. Those of us who work daily with him know that this joy is not cosmetic but flows from an inner stream, consistent and infectious. His secret is that he manifestly lives with the One in whose presence is fullness of joy and at whose right hand are pleasures for evermore.

The world will be a richer place if all who read this book follow his example and learn to jump for joy.

TERRY VIRGO

Preface

While writing this book on joy it has been an eye-opener for me to discover how scant the literature upon this theme is. In fact there is hardly any. There are several books which have 'joy' in the title, but invariably the title bears little or no relationship to the subject-matter. This is an astonishing fact when you consider the large place given to joy in the Bible and which it ought to have in the lives of Christian believers. I have written in the hope that God will use the book to lead many Christians to desire to be filled with all joy and peace in believing. For too long we have misrepresented God by giving the impression that the Christian life is a drab and dreary experience, and the man of the world looks on and thinks that, of all men, we are the most miserable. But, fellowshipping with the risen Christ, we ought to be—of all people—the most happy.

One of the many reasons we need revival is because such an outpouring of the Holy Spirit would restore to the church not only the amazing power of God but also that supernatural joy which is everywhere in evidence in the life of the early church, a demonstration of the truth that 'the kingdom of God is . . . righteousness, peace and joy in the Holy Spirit' (Rom 14:17, NIV).

I have found that many joys come to me through friends and I am grateful to Arnold Bell who kindly read and corrected proofs and to Phil Stanton for his willing help and observations. Many thanks, too, to Pam Haworth who typed the manuscript and is, in our busy office, a shining example of longsuffering with joy. I am indebted to my dear friend, Terry Virgo, for kindly writing the foreword. It is one of the joys of my life to work alongside him here in our home church at Clarendon and in the wider ministry among the churches at home and overseas.

Finally, my thanks to my beloved wife, Dorothy, whose support, love and powerful intercessions for me and the ministry that God has given me never fail.

HENRY TYLER

I

God of Joy

'I just want to be happy.' This is the longing of most people. It is a desire that is understandable, for God created us to be happy. The world was a supremely happy place until man yielded to sin. Since sin entered nothing has been the same, for sin marred everything that God had originally made good. And now happiness in this fallen world has an elusive quality about it. Should you find it you do not know how long you will have it. For happiness, as the word itself indicates, is dependent on life's happenings—its swiftly changing events can bring drastic changes in our fortunes. There are times when all is going well and we could even say, 'We've never had it so good!' But then something happens and our whole situation is changed. We may be made re-dundant and lose our job or we may become ill or we fail to achieve what we have set our hearts upon; we suffer bereavement or divorce and the sunshine of happiness has gone and our lives are clouded and overcast.

Yet there remains in the human heart a universal desire to be happy. And here is man's dilemma: he wants to be happy but he knows that all human happiness is vulnerable, continually threatened by sudden change that will bring it to a swift and certain end. Most of us, stoically, try to make the best of a bad job ever hoping that the good times will last. But the threat remains and the truth is we have no answer to the problem.

Upon the dilemma and darkness of man the light of the glorious gospel breaks in, bringing glad tidings of great joy. Joy is superior to happiness as it is in no way derived from or dependent upon what happens in this world. It is the gift of God. His joy will enhance our days when things are good and we have all that we desire, but it will not desert us when, with a sudden shock, life deals us some cruel blow or devastating experience, for this unchanging joy comes from our unchanging God.

But what *is* joy? What do we mean by the term? Amazingly, though the Bible has such a lot to say about joy, definitions are hard to find, both in the Bible and in commentaries upon it. God is the God of all grace—'grace that does everything for man who deserves nothing', and joy is at the heart of grace. Grace is God saving sinful man. Joy is his delight and pleasure in doing so. This he shares with the sinner he saves. In the Greek the word for grace is *charis* and for joy the word is *chara*—these show clearly their affinity with each other. Where grace comes it brings the joy of the Lord and as we ask for and receive more grace we experience more joy. Joy is that irresistible quality which lustres all life's events with the superlative bliss of God's presence and favour.

God the source of joy

God is the centre and sphere of all true joy, for joy finds its origin in him: 'in [his] presence there is fullness of joy, in [his] right hand are pleasures for evermore' (Ps 16:11, RSV). The psalmist speaks of God as 'God, my exceeding joy' (Ps 43:4)— exceeding our greatest expectations, exceeding all other delights. God himself, then, is the fountain of joy. Such joy is constant, for it flows from a perennial fountain. It never freezes in winter or dries up in summer. For God and his attributes are eternal. Lesser joys cannot and will not last. They are but for a season. But *this* joy is for ever.

God the creator of joy

God created the world in joy. The Bible opens with the words 'In the beginning God created the heavens and the earth . . .' and then goes on to explain how the earth was without form and empty until the Spirit of God moved on the face of the deep and, out of the chaos, there came forth a new creation. As each separate work of creation was completed, God saw that it was good. For all his works are perfect and his handiwork in creation was of such superlative beauty that 'the morning stars sang together, and all the sons of God shouted for joy' (Job 38:7).

The world, then, was created in joy and celebrated with joy—joy in what God had done and the way he had done it; joy in the power that God put forth when he spoke and it was done; joy in the finished product; and joy in the One by whom all things were made—the eternal Word, the everlasting Son of the Father, dwelling in his bosom from all eternity. For all things were made by him and for him (Col 1:16). What a tremendous statement that is! The mountains in their solidity and grandeur were made by him and made for him to stand throughout the ages of time to be the Father's tribute to his Son. The humblest flower that grows was not born to 'waste its sweetness on the desert air' but was made for him—to pour forth its perfume as incense to the praise of Jesus. No wonder there was singing and shouting from the angelic powers. The joy of angels knows no bounds when the King of angels is exalted.

God encompassed by joy

The angels are seen in Scripture to be creatures of joy and they encompass the throne of God. They stand in the presence of God, and that's where there is fullness of joy. Jesus declared that there was joy in the presence of the angels of God, and we learn that they are sent forth to minister to us, who are the heirs of salvation. They come to bring messages of joy from God to men, as at the birth of Jesus when they brought the 'glad tidings of great joy'. For when God brought his first-born into the world he said, 'Let all the angels of God worship him' (Heb 1:6). And the Bible reminds us that when we come to God, the judge of all, and to

Jesus, the mediator of the new covenant and to the blood of sprinkling which he shed and to the general assembly and church of the first-born, we come, too, to an innumerable company of angels in joyful assembly (or, as it can be rendered, in festal array). These burning intelligences who exist solely to do the will of God are possessed of such joy that they continually keep high festival. For God is surrounded by angels of joy—myriads of angels—in an eternal convocation of joy. This is the company that God keeps, and when the Lord Jesus taught us to pray that God's will 'be done on earth as it is in heaven', he meant that men should emulate the angels in worshipping and obeying God and doing so with exceeding joy.

Rejoicing before God

If the joy of angels is an example for men and women to follow, we can see God's purpose in his dealings with Israel in instituting great feasts which were at the very heart of their national life and identity. These feasts were commanded by God to take place at certain times throughout the year when all the people were together for the express purpose of rejoicing before the Lord. Deuteronomy 16 speaks of these great national festivals when all were called to celebrate the goodness of God with offerings and thank-offerings. What times of unparalleled joy these must have been as, with their families and friends, the people celebrated the goodness of the Lord. Their songs of joy must have filled the air—'Sing unto God, sing praises to his name: extol him that rideth upon the heavens . . . and rejoice before him' (Ps 68:4, AV). It would seem too that the regularity of these special feasts was intended to instil into the people the privilege of *always* rejoicing: 'you shall rejoice before the Lord your God in *all* your undertakings' (Deut 12:18).

An astounding example of what it means to rejoice before the Lord is found in Proverbs chapter 8. This is a chapter devoted to the theme of wisdom, only here wisdom is personified. The account is put in the first person singular, and many believers in all ages have seen this as referring to the Lord Jesus Christ existing in eternal glory and union with the Father and the Spirit, before his coming to earth as man.

What an amazing scene is set before us here! Having declared 'I was there' before the world was created, verses 30–31 go on to state, 'I was beside Him as a master workman; and I was daily His delight, rejoicing always before Him, rejoicing in the world, His earth, and having my delight in the sons of men.' The word here rendered 're-joicing' is an interesting one, as sometimes it is translated 'laughing'. Sometimes it means 'to play' or 'to sport'.

What a revelation this gives of rejoicing before the Lord, and what an example to follow!

God wants his people to be joyful. You cannot possibly miss this in the Bible. God's plan for people is that they should know joy. Both the Old and the New Testaments abound with the command to rejoice. Frequently God shares with his people his plans to bless them and how, in believing and obeying him, their joys will abound:

> Hear the word of the Lord, O nations . . . and say,
> 'He who scattered Israel will gather him . . .' For the
> Lord has ransomed Jacob, and redeemed him from
> the hand of him who was stronger than he. 'And
> they shall come and shout for joy on the height of
> Zion, and they shall be radiant over the bounty
> [goodness] of the Lord . . . Then the virgin shall
> rejoice in the dance, and the young men and the old,
> together, for I will turn their mourning into joy, and
> will comfort them, and give them joy for their
> sorrow' (Jer 31:10–13).

Likewise, the evidence of God's judgement is seen when he says of the disobedient, 'Then I will make to cease from the cities of Judah and from the streets of Jerusalem the voice of joy and the voice of gladness . . . the land will become a ruin' (Jer 7:34). In other words, God is saying, 'There is no joy for those who depart from me.' And when in mercy he restores his people's fortunes again, turning their captivity, we read that their mouths will be filled with laughter and their lips with singing, 'The ransomed of the Lord return, and everlasting joy will be on their heads' (Is 51:11).

In the New Testament God's purpose and provision to bring us into joy and keep us in joy are everywhere in evidence. For example, Jesus prays that we might know 'the full measure of [his] joy' (Jn 17:13, NIV). In Paul's prayer in Romans 15, inspired by the Spirit of God, he prays for the believers there to be *filled* with joy (verse 13). It is not God's way to deal in half measures. He desires to pour such joy into our lives that like the water pots at Cana we shall be filled to the brim, and every part of our being shall be permeated and saturated with joy, overflowing with delight in him. He wants us to be filled with *all* joy, knowing all the varieties of joy that emanate from him— the heavenly joys of reconciliation and fellowship with the Father and his Son; the joys that are found in the Holy Spirit, enabling and empowering us to do the work of God; the human joys that enrich and bless our lives. God wants us to know them to the full. Settle it in your heart that God wants you to live a life filled with joy. Well, how can that be?

God himself our joy

It is as we know God that we know joy. To realize that the all mighty and all holy God is my Father —loving, caring, warm and welcoming, always glad to see me, to meet me and bless me—is both a never-ending source of wonder and a never-ending source of joy. Even the believers living in Old Testament times reached such heights of joy in their fellowship with God that they would say, 'Besides Thee, I desire nothing on earth.' They found such joy in God that they reckoned there was absolutely nothing on earth to compare or compete with it.

Robert Murray M'Cheyne recorded in his diary: 'Rose early to seek God, and found Him whom my soul loves. Who would not rise early to meet such company?'[1] Yes, and many another has testified that in such company—Father, Son and Holy Spirit—is found 'the best bliss that earth affords'. One of the great privileges as believers is that we have access to the Father through the Lord Jesus by the Holy Spirit. Here is incomparable joy: to meet with the God of joy, to delight myself in him, to see by faith the glory of God in the face of Jesus Christ, to be ravished anew by his reconciling love, to realize that there is no condemnation in Christ—I am cleansed, forgiven, made fit for God's presence—to be assured by the powerful ministry of the Holy Spirit that I am accepted in the Beloved, that the welcome I received when I first came to Christ is renewed every time I come. The voice that drew me then, draws me now: 'the one who comes to Me, I will certainly not cast out' (Jn 6:37). And in coming I meet with the overwhelming love of God in Christ and my heart is flooded with joy.

Rejoicing with God

In such a fellowship we shall discover that we can rejoice *with* God. We shall find that God loves to share his heart and his plans with his people that we may rejoice together in what he has purposed to do. The prophetic word recorded in Isaiah 65:17 is clear and sure: 'I create new heavens and a new earth'—that is what God will do. The prophecy continues, 'be glad and rejoice for ever in what I create; for behold, I create Jerusalem for rejoicing, and her people for gladness'. God goes on to say, '*I* will also rejoice in Jerusalem and be glad in My people.' So we see here a mutual rejoicing. God brings his people into joy and he himself rejoices to do so. Just as Jesus said in the parable of the lost sheep, 'Rejoice with me,' so we shall discover that God calls us to rejoice with him not only in the recovery of the lost but in the building of his church, at the ever-expanding increase of his kingdom and, at the last, his complete and ultimate triumph when we shall be invited to 'enter into the joy of [our] master' (Mt 25:21, 24).

God rejoicing over you

The joy and delight is not all on one side. We can rejoice in God and with God. But God also delights in us.

Zephaniah is an Old Testament prophecy heavy with wrath and judgement. But judgement is not the whole story, for God delights in mercy, so the book concludes with a marvellous prophecy of God's intention to restore Jerusalem. In anticipation of that glad day God calls his people to shout for joy, to rejoice and exult with all their hearts. But then the prophecy goes on to apply the same actions to God himself. He too will exult and rejoice with shouts of joy. But *his* rejoicing is over *them*. He takes sheer delight in them and what he will do for them. This is the God with whom we have to do. He will rest us in his love and rejoice over us with singing.

Many need to have their eyes opened by the Holy Spirit to see how the Lord delights in his saints and takes pleasure in his people. They are his special treasure and the apple of his eye. When Israel was smarting under the Babylonian yoke, God foretold through his servant Jeremiah that he would break the power of Babylon, that he would restore the fortunes of his people. He would bring them back and turn their mourning into joy and make an everlasting covenant with them, putting godly fear in their hearts. One amazing blessing after another is promised. Again and again the words come, 'I will . . . I will . . . I will.' But the crowning blessing is this—when God says: 'And I will rejoice to do them good' (Jer 32:41). That is the heart of God—rejoicing over you. You don't believe it? Read Isaiah 62:5: 'As the bridegroom rejoices over the bride, so your God will rejoice over you.'

Thus, before ever we consider the grounds of our own joy, we see that, first and foremost, God is rejoicing over us, his new creation in Christ.

Perhaps we see God's own joy more clearly revealed in the life of Jesus, and it is therefore to this that we now turn.

2

Man of Joy

One of the greatest insights we have concerning the Lord Jesus Christ is the prophecy in Psalm 45:7—'God, Thy God has anointed Thee with the oil of joy above Thy fellows.' This is quoted in the letter to the Hebrews, highlighting its importance. If the statement means anything at all it means that Jesus had more joy than any other man. In other words, he was the happiest man that ever lived. But this is not the way most of us think of the Lord Jesus. Indeed, this is not at all the general impression that has come down to us via Christian tradition. Artists, writers and preachers all generally have conveyed the picture of a sad and sometimes even gloomy personality. No doubt their intention was to present us with a man serious in purpose. But seriousness and sadness are not the same thing and should never be confused. To be sober, to use another biblical term, means to be serious and self-controlled. It does not mean to be sombre, which the dictionary defines as dark, gloomy and dismal. Had we given due weight to the fact that Jesus walked on earth with the superabundant anointing of joy in the Holy Spirit, we would reject out of hand the notion of a Christ whose view of life was one long, hard, terrible trial and burden. We would refuse to sing of him:

> Lone and dreary, faint and weary,
> Through the desert thou didst go.

Weary he may have been, but dreary—never! He had dealt the devil a body blow by refusing point-blank all his suggestions in the wilderness. He was not in the least dreary. It is the most exhilarating experience to defeat the devil, and in the power of the Spirit that's just what Jesus did.

Man of sorrows

But some will say Jesus was a man of sorrows. Yes, certainly Scripture gives him this designation in one single place—Isaiah 53:3—'a man of sorrows, and acquainted with grief'. But the context (v.4) makes it clear that he *carried our* sorrows. The prophecy declares that Christ would bear our sins on the cross, dealing with them in their entirety. The whole of our human burden—sin and the sorrow that it brings, the ruin and the wreckage that it has brought in its train—Jesus took up; he took our infirmities and carried our sorrow. It is in *this* sense that he was a man of sorrows. It was part of his great sacrifice. But having no sin of his own, Jesus lived in unclouded fellowship with the Father, knowing in his sinless walk with God more of true happiness than any other man that ever lived. In common with all mankind he had to face the shocks and strains of life. We all pass through times of sorrow and Jesus was not exempt from these. But even in them, the rich anointing of the oil of gladness was the dominant characteristic of his life.

It is sometimes pointed out that though we read in the gospels that Jesus wept, we never read that he laughed. But then there are many things that Jesus did that are not recorded in the New Testament, yet we know that he did them simply because he was a man. Many of us, I feel, have yet to get to grips with what that really means. Bible-believers would not hesitate to confess the creed—that Jesus Christ was very God of very God, and yet truly man. But we have great difficulty in working out the practical implications that that statement brings. The breathtaking truth is that the eternal Son of the Father—the second person in the holy trinity, co-equal with the Father and the Spirit and with them One God for ever—took our human nature in a body of human flesh and was made like us in all things. He did not pretend to be a man. He was not acting a part—a mere actor appearing for a while on the world's stage. He really became man, made like us in all things except our sin. That difference is, of course, of crucial importance and has far reaching conse-quences. But it is the *only* difference.

So, when I hear people say, 'You never read in the New Testament that Jesus laughed,' my reply is that, as true man, he must have done so. We do not read that Jesus ever attended to the normal

bodily functions that we associate with going to
the toilet, though in his teaching he makes reference to this (Mt 15:17). But, being a man with
bowels and a bladder, we know that these normal
functions must have been part of his daily routine. It sometimes takes the shock of such earthi-
ness to bring home to our hearts the outstanding
glory of the incarnation. But many of us struggle
to accept the humanness of Jesus.

One of the first heresies that the church had to
deal with was Docetism, that is, the teaching that
Jesus was not really a man but that he just had the
appearance of a man. This teaching emerged in
New Testament times and came to its zenith in the
second century. John, in his first epistle, says that
it is the spirit of antichrist to deny that 'Jesus
Christ has come in the flesh' (1 Jn 4:2–3). Let us
not shy away from the truth that Jesus was
thoroughly human, truly a man—God manifest in
the flesh.

That means, first of all, that he shared our
human joy. He spoke of the children at play as
they imitated life's happenings around them,
finding pleasure in the pretence of playing wed-
dings and funerals. As a normal child, Jesus
would naturally have joined in these games himself and, as one who grew in wisdom and stature
and in favour with God and man, we can only
glean that he was a very popular lad. In later years
we see him as a good mixer, ready to mingle with
some extraordinary types—a friend of tax-
gatherers and sinners, a man ready to take the
little children on his knees and cuddle them in his
arms. There was something very warm, winsome

and sunny about his personality. Even a woman with a shady reputation felt that she should come and wash his feet with her tears, towel them with her hair and, with an amazing show of affection, kiss his feet. Jesus' own comment on this was: '. . . this woman, from the time I entered, has not stopped kissing my feet' (Lk 7:45, NIV). Many are the lessons we can learn from this incident, but what shines through most conspicuously is the full, warm humanity of Jesus, ever giving out his love. He shows that he could receive love in such an outflow of affection and from such a woman. We see too that he felt the slight of Simon the Pharisee, who had failed to provide him with the ordinary, usual courtesies always given to an invited guest. Shown such rudeness, the love the woman gave was all the more appreciated and welcomed. Yes, he was very human!

Another feature of his mixing with mankind is seen in his delight in taking meals with others. Jesus was no loner, neither was he an ascetic. Rather he gained the reputation of being a gluttonous man and a drunkard (Lk 7:34). This we know was not true but what *was* true was that the Son of man came eating and drinking—that is to say, he enjoyed socializing and spending time with others over a meal. This was part of his lifestyle. We see him at table at Simon's house, at Levi's party, with Martha and Mary at their home in Bethany and with his disciples at the wedding in Cana. What a time of merrymaking these Jewish marriage celebrations were, with their feasting and freely flowing wine, with the music and dancing! You must not imagine that the friend of sinners would stand aloof from the joyous goings-on. He was not content to be a mere spectator. He would not be a wallflower. No, he would have shared in the delight of those lovely Israeli dances, caught up with the whole community in celebrating the joy of the bride and the bridegroom. Jesus reveals his acquaintance with and approval of these human celebrations of happiness when, in telling the matchless story of the homecoming of the prodigal son, he says they made merry with a banquet and with music and dancing. In times of great joy this is a perfectly natural thing to do.

If you are concerned about living a life of joy you could start by being natural, sharing the ordinary joys of ordinary people, mixing more with them, rejoicing with them in their marriage, in the birth of their baby or their recovery from illness, in their success at examinations. Don't run away with the idea that to please God you must always be doing 'spiritual things'. Look at the Son of man. He was not always preaching. Sometimes he was at the party! But always and everywhere, he was about his Father's business. Be a Son of man too. In other words, be natural—be human.

A marvellous friend

Our Lord's capacity for friendship is seen supremely in his relationship with his own disciples. He did not call them servants but friends. He was wholly committed to them and called them to be wholly involved with him. He brought them in on all his plans and activities. He trained them and empowered them to share his ministry among the people. When the pressure of the work increased, he would take them aside to a quiet place for some rest. They reclined with him at meal times, so marvellously relaxed that John felt free to position his head on the body of Jesus. Yes, he actually heard the heartbeat of the world's redeemer! I love to imagine their camaraderie as they walked through the corn fields together, saw the miracles that Jesus did, shared the astonishment and joy of the crowds as the lame were made to walk and the blind to see. How proud they must have been! This man was their friend! And if it is true, as I am sure it is, that the best friend to have is the one who knows the worst about you yet loves you just the same, these men surely knew the love of such a friend in spite of their weaknesses, failures and unbelief. One of them has testified of Jesus: 'having loved His own who were in the world, He loved them to the end' (Jn 13:1). There was never any breakdown in his love for them and there never would be.

John's gospel closes with an amazing scene—Jesus, risen from the dead, seeks out his own men. He knows exactly where to find them so he makes his way to the beach. I wonder how many times he had met them there—to picnic, to swim and to enjoy one another's fellowship. Now he calls to them with a question. We may paraphrase it—'You haven't had any success, have you?' Their answer is a decided no! For the night's fishing has not yielded any catch whatsoever. Jesus says, 'Put the net on the right side of the boat and you will find.' What they find is staggering. They catch so many fish, they literally stagger to bring them to land. On the beach a charcoal fire is burning, fish is cooking and some of the freshly caught fish are added to what is already there. Then the Lord gives the invitation, 'Come, and dine.' The mighty conqueror of sin and death celebrates his resurrection and reunion with his friends—not with a praise meeting but with a barbecue. What a man! What a Saviour! One moment he works a miracle and the next he prepares breakfast for his friends.

Anointed with joy

But above and beyond such human joys, Jesus knew as a man a rich anointing of joy in the Spirit. Many men have, in all generations, known joy in God but Jesus knew it in a measure unknown to any other. Some of the believers of whom we read in the past, when blessed with large effusions of the Spirit of joy, have found it more than they could bear and found the joy all too overwhelming for their human constitution. 'Oh God, stay your hand!' cried D. L. Moody.[2] But Jesus, moving in unsullied fellowship with God, contained all that. The joy of the Lord flowed like a river, constantly replenishing his whole being.

He was always full and at times so full that the river of joy overflowed its banks. So, after the seventy-two return from mission, we read, 'At that very time [Jesus] rejoiced greatly in the Holy Spirit' (Lk 10:21) and he poured forth his praises and thanksgiving to his Father, the Lord of heaven and earth. Wescott, in his commentary on Hebrews, commenting on Christ's prolific anointing with joy, says it refers not to the solemn anointing to royal dignity but to the festive anointings on occasions of rejoicing.[3] So it was a festival of joy in this day when Jesus contemplated Satan's downfall; demons cast out by his disciples; their names recorded in heaven; revelation given to ordinary, unlearned men and all things given by the Father to the Son. It was these facts, impressed by the Spirit, that caused the Saviour to overflow with joy.

Jesus, we have seen, mixed with men to share their human joys, but as man he mixed with God, delighting himself in the Father, never doing anything that would displease him, guarding his fellowship with God, loving righteousness and hating iniquity. He walked the tightrope of being in this sinful world, mixing with sinners yet never yielding to sin. And God blessed him by giving him the Spirit without measure, evident in a surplus of joy.

And he longs for us to know it too. He reveals the secret to all who want to know a life of joy: 'If you keep My commandments, you will abide in My love; just as I have kept My Father's commandments, and abide in His love. These things I have spoken to you that My joy may be in you, and that your joy may be full' (Jn 15:10–11). The way to a life of joy is by a life of holiness. But what is holiness? Holiness is a life filled with God and thrilled with God. Holiness will not make you less human; it will make you more truly human—like Jesus, who was so fully a Son of man *and* a man of joy.

3
Spirit of Joy

The Spirit we speak of is the Holy Spirit. We have seen in the life of Jesus that his anointing with joy was vitally connected with his holy life. He loved righteousness and hated iniquity. He was a man with a passion to please God and he was the happiest man alive. So holiness and joy are not mutually exclusive—no, indeed, holiness is the way to true happiness. If we think otherwise it means we have either a distorted view of holiness or, for that matter, a distorted view of joy. For in the Spirit of God both holiness and joy are evident in his being and in his ministry. Wherever he comes he creates holiness and joy, so we read that the disciples were *continually filled* with joy and with the Holy Spirit (Acts 13:52).

The fruit of the Spirit

The fruit of the Spirit (Gal 5:22–23) is joy, and the fruit is always determined by the root. The bringer of joy is a being of joy. When the Thessalonians heard Paul preach, he records the fact that they 'received the word in much tribulation with the joy of the Holy Spirit' (1 Thess 1:6). The last clause speaks both of the joy which the Holy Spirit has in himself and the joy he imparts to those who believe.

It has been frequently pointed out that the word used by Paul in Galatians 5:22 is not the *plural* 'fruits' but the *singular* 'fruit'. There is a wise purpose in this for this is fruit in a cluster and we must not separate what God has joined together. It is foolish for anyone to think that they can obtain joy independently of the other virtues listed here; each is vitally connected to the others. The Spirit comes to produce all these Christlike characteristics in our lives. I cannot, therefore, know joy in its fullness if I am not loving—loving God and loving my neighbour. I *cannot* know joy unless I know peace—peace with God, with others and with myself. I *will not* know peace without self-control. So we learn that by the Spirit's indwelling God's desire is to create in us the many-splendoured loveliness of Christ. In one sense, Christ *is* the fruit of the Spirit, and the more I become like Jesus the more I shall know of joy.

The chief ministry of the Spirit

The supreme ministry of the Holy Spirit is to glorify the Lord Jesus and it is by this means that he brings joy to our hearts. He takes the things of Christ and shows them to us. This is the Spirit that searches all things, the 'deep things of God'. He scans the depths of deity and what he sees he shows to us. This makes the Saviour to be more marvellous in our eyes, our appreciation grows and our love increases. He quickens our faith to know the presence of Jesus and at times we perceive our risen Lord to be so powerfully near that the tide of joy in our hearts is at the flood and overflowing. It was this aspect of the Holy Spirit's ministry which Peter described in his letter when he said 'though you have not seen Him, you love Him, and though you do not see Him now, but believe in Him, you greatly rejoice with joy inexpressible and full of glory' (1 Pet 1:8). This is what it means to rejoice in the Lord. Whatever else may be happening or not happening in the world around us, our hearts are continually knowing a fresh revelation of the risen Christ by his Spirit. This ravishes our hearts afresh with his love, anoints our eyes again to see what he is seeing and empowers us to do what he is doing.

The Spirit's manifestation

The Spirit brings us joy, too, as he manifests his gifts. In his first letter to the Thessalonians Paul states that God's will for us is to rejoice always, to pray without ceasing and in everything give thanks (1 Thess 5:16–18). He immediately follows this with a strong prohibition—'Do not quench the Spirit; do not despise *prophetic utterances* [margin: "*gifts*"]' (v.19). So we discern a strong connection between the joy of believers and the exercise of the Spirit's gifts. The spontaneous utterance given by a member of the body of Christ in the public assembly for their encouragement, consolation or building up is not to be despised, for that would be quenching the Spirit. We know from 1 Corinthians 12:7 that it is through the exercise of the supernatural gifts of God that the invisible Spirit of God manifests himself in the body. These gifts are not optionals. They are not luxuries but necessities for the well-being of the body. They are not given to inflate the ego of any one individual but to inspire and bless the whole worshipping community. To despise prophecy or any other of the Spirit's gifts is to pit my will against the sovereign Spirit, who does as *he* wills. To despise prophecy given by an ordinary member of the body is to stamp out the flame of the Spirit's love in that member's heart—a flame ignited by the Holy Spirit in order that some strong word of consolation and love may break over the whole gathered people of God.

Prophecy should be weighed but never despised. To despise such utterances means we rob the body of Christ of that word and of the love and the joy that word brings. The same principle applies to any of the gifts, whether gifts of utterance and insight such as prophecy, discerning of spirits, tongues and their interpretation, words of wisdom, words of knowledge, or whether gifts of ability; faith to believe for the impossible, faith to accomplish the impossible, the working of miracles and healings. For whatever gift is exercised, though the gifts differ they are given by the one Spirit and he manifests his presence through them.

We must be very careful then how we handle the gifts for, in despising them, we dishonour the Spirit himself. It is no task of a leader of worship to 'put out the Spirit's fire' (1 Thess 5:19, NIV). The one longing of our hearts should be to have the Holy Spirit's presence and to have him *manifestly* present. We are therefore very foolish indeed to resist, oppose or neglect the exercise of spiritual gifts. In this matter our souls must be captive to the written word of God, for to despise prophesying is to quench the Spirit and to restrict the flow of joy.

This is inevitably the case, for all the gifts of the Spirit display one or more of the attributes of God. For instance, God is omniscient—that is, he knows all things. This is evident when the Spirit speaks in prophecy or with a word of knowledge or wisdom or gives the source and identity of spirits. He can reveal something that happened in the past long ago or in the recent past. He can expose the present situation of any person, sometimes disclosing their thoughts which no one else could possibly know. He can see and speak of the future, causing his people to abound in hope. To be confronted with such utterances is to know that God knows all things and he is present with us.

Sometimes it is the omnipotence of God that is manifested by way of miracles and healings. How ready the Spirit of God is to show us that the things impossible with men are possible with God! Whether the Spirit manifests the wisdom of God or the power of God, his omnipresence becomes more than a doctrine—it becomes a living, bright reality. Paul expresses it so vividly when, describing the early gatherings in the Corinthian church, he speaks of prophesying and its effects, saying how the unbeliever enters and he 'is convicted by all, he is called to account by all; the secrets of his heart are disclosed; and so he will fall on his face and worship God, declaring that God is certainly among you'.

Special seasons of joy

Both the Bible and the experience of Christians testify to the fact that the Holy Spirit grants special times or seasons of joy. Peter indicates in his preaching (Acts 3:19–20) that up to the coming again of the Lord Jesus we may expect special visitations of the Spirit upon the church. We know from church history that again and again God has intervened in remarkable spiritual power when the church has declined in influence and godliness. God has graciously sent revival which has been like the season of spring after a long, cold winter—new life breaks forth everywhere. Individual believers have likewise known extraordinary operations of the Holy Spirit overwhelming their hearts with the reality of Christ's presence, sending wave after wave of divine love, giving them to know in experience the enigma of which Paul speaks when writing to the Ephesians—'the love of Christ which surpasses knowledge' (Eph 3:19). Their joy has been raised to a degree and dimension truly out of this world—a joy unutterable and full of glory. Dr Martyn Lloyd-Jones in his book *Joy Unspeakable* (Kingsway Publications 1984) has rendered the church a great service in collating an array of evidence from Christian biographies of men and women who, longing to know more of God, have prayed and known the Spirit of God coming upon them. They have been lifted to heights of rapture they could not adequately express or explain. For some there was a great reluctance even to speak of their experiences, feeling that they were too sacred to mention. Such experiences find a parallel in the life of the Lord Jesus, to which we have already referred: 'At that very time [Jesus] rejoiced greatly in the Holy Spirit' (Lk10:21). It was obviously a special season of joy when the joy he already knew was increased and intensified.

I call attention to this aspect of the Spirit's ministry because there is always that tendency in our hearts to settle for what we have when we should be reaching for more. Let us be hungry for God. Whatever we have known of the Spirit's help and enablings in the past, let us never think that we have reached finality. Believe for more.

There is a word which has faded from usage among Christian believers; we sometimes come across it in the old writers and certainly in the old hymns. It is the word 'rapture'. Mention that word today and it carries the connotation of something that happens when Christ returns in glory, but we are referring to what can be known here and now when the Spirit of God comes to a man and overwhelms him with God's love so that he feels and senses that love to such a degree it raises him to ecstasy in God and in God alone. As Wesley wrote of it:

> O the rapturous height
> Of the holy delight
> Which I felt in the life-giving blood!
> Of my Saviour possessed
> I was perfectly blessed
> As if filled with the fullness of God.

We can know seasons with such an excess of delight that we shall cry out with the Scottish preacher, John Welch: 'Hold, Lord, hold! It is enough! Remember that I am but an earthen vessel and if I have too much of glory I shall not live.' In such times our joy knows no bounds and our natural constitution needs supernatural enabling to cope with such excessive delight. I think it is unwise to give a name or designation to such experiences. That is why I have deliberately written this section under the heading '*special* seasons of joy'. Suffice to say that this has been the experience of believers from different backgrounds and of different temperaments. Yet one discerns a common characteristic: they were people who ever hungered for God himself. They were marked by holiness, humility and prayer.

If you have been born again of the Spirit that is wonderful. But remember, that is only the beginning. There is more. If you have been baptized in the Holy Spirit—praise God! But remember, there is more. Whatever you have known of the powerful operations of the Spirit in the past, yet there is more. More power, more grace, more holiness . . . more joy.

4

The Joy of Salvation

How can we know the life of joy for ourselves? First, we must know the joy of salvation. The gospel is good news and it broke upon this dark world with the angelic announcement, 'I bring you good news of a great joy which shall be for all the people' (Lk 2:10). Where the gospel is truly believed it produces great joy. It was so when Paul preached at Thessalonica and also when Philip was evangelizing in Samaria. Souls were saved, bodies healed and demons cast out. No small wonder then that we read 'there was much rejoicing in that city' (Acts 7:8).

The fact of the matter is that joyless Christians and, likewise, joyless churches are contradictions in terms. Yet in these days we meet with both all too frequently. Some have been in this joyless condition for so long that they now regard it as the norm. And if by chance they should meet with a believer so happy in God he is rejoicing with 'joy inexpressible and full of glory' (1 Pet 1:8), they look askance at such an abnormality! What was normal in the New Testament is abnormal to those who have settled for sub-scriptural standards. Indeed, you get the impression from some that they think the more miserable you are, the more holy you are! Such people should take a fresh look at the message of salvation. It is *good* news and it brings *great* joy. If we have disbelieved or distorted the gospel, we shall never know the joy it brings.

I find when dealing with people who sense a lack of joy in their lives that many have never had a clear view of the gospel. There has been a failure to understand what Christ has done for those who believe in him. The Bible clearly reveals that our glorious Saviour in his death on the cross has fully satisfied the just claims of a holy God. The law has no outstanding claims against the believer. Every one of those claims has been fully discharged by the Lord Jesus. Our sins and their appalling consequences have effectively and eternally been banished by the blood of the Lamb of God.

Christ, then, has done the work. He has done it alone and he has done it entirely. God has accepted the sacrifice and declared it by raising Jesus from the dead. When we put our trust in him our sins are forgiven and our sins are forgotten, for God says, 'I will remember [them] no more' (Jer 31:34). To rest in such a revelation provides the solid basis for a life of joy.

John Bunyan wonderfully expresses this in *Pilgrim's Progress* when he describes how Christian lost his burden of sin:

He ran . . . till he came at a place somewhat ascending; and upon that place stood a cross, and a little below, in the bottom, a sepulchre. So I saw in my dream, that just as Christian came up with the cross, his burden loosed from off his shoulders, and fell from off his back, and began to tumble, and so continued to do till it came to the mouth of the sepulchre, where it fell in, and I saw it no more.

Then was Christian glad and lightsome, and said with a merry heart, 'He hath given me rest by His sorrow, and life by His death.' . . . Then Christian gave three leaps for joy, and went his way singing . . .[4]

You can afford to be 'glad and lightsome' and in every way 'merry of heart' when you know that your sins are gone. You can 'leap for joy' in the realization that you are ransomed, healed, restored, forgiven. When the Holy Spirit witnesses with our spirits that we are the children of God, it is enough to make us delirious with delight. It is a thousand pities that so many stop short of this and so fail to partake of such joy. Many never get beyond repentance.

It is, of course, essential that we repent of our sins. That is absolutely vital. But Jesus taught that true repentance leads to the knowledge of sins forgiven (Lk 24:47) and Luke also indicates that such forgiveness leads us to great joy (Lk 24:52). This can be demonstrated from many places in the Bible. For instance, in the time of Nehemiah we read of Ezra reading the law of God to the people; the word came with such melting power to their hearts that they were overwhelmed by it. We read that 'all the people were weeping when they heard the words of the law' (Neh 8:9). This comes as no surprise when we remember that the law exposes us all as guilty before God and makes it very clear that we are under its curse and can in no way extricate ourselves from its condemnation.

Nehemiah and Ezra had further teaching for these weeping people and the word they brought from God brought about a complete transformation among them. They told them not to weep, not to mourn, but rather to go and make a great celebration. Two reasons were given for this instruction (Neh 8:9–11). First, the day was holy to the Lord, so holiness is not to be equated with sadness, even less with gloominess. On this holy day mourning and weeping were totally inappropriate. The second reason is enshrined in the well-known words, 'The joy of the Lord is your strength [or stronghold].' From this statement we learn that though all the people were smitten by sorrow, devastated by the condemning power of the law, the Lord had joy in his heart and he wanted his people to share it and to share it immediately. Why should the Lord have joy in his heart when his people had sorrow in theirs? The only answer must be that the Lord, in seeing their sorrow, knew it to be godly sorrow that leads to repentance (cf. 2 Cor 7:10, NIV), and repentance in man brings joy to God. The Lord Jesus taught us that there is joy in the presence of the angels of God over one sinner who repents and, in those matchless parables recorded in Luke's gospel, he indicates that it is Father himself who initiates that joy: 'Rejoice with me, for I have found my sheep which was lost!' (Lk 15:6).

If we could really comprehend the magnitude

of what God has done for us through our Lord Jesus Christ—loosed us from our sins, brought us out of darkness, delivered us from Satan's dominion, indwelt and empowered us by his Spirit, made us heirs of God and joint heirs with Christ— if we really appreciated this, we should be ecstatic with joy. But whether we are or not, God is! It is his chief glory and joy to seek the lost and save them with an everlasting salvation.

This, then, is the joy of the Lord and it is our stronghold and security. So Nehemiah's instruction to this repentant people is 'stop weeping, start rejoicing, make a great mirth'. God called them to make a quick, almost abrupt, change from one emotion to the other. They were not to think that they needed a prolonged period of probation—and certainly not one of penance. Without any delay, the repentant heart is invited to participate in the joy of the Lord—just as when the prodigal son returned to his father, he said to the servants, 'Quickly bring out the best robe and put it on him, and put a ring on his hand and sandals on his feet and bring the fatted calf, kill it, and let us eat and be merry'—so they made a great mirth!

The religious mind sees it differently, thinking it much more appropriate to have a solemn litany for the penitent so that after a prolonged season of sorrow the sinner can pay his way back to favour with the currency of grief. Grace operates on a different level altogether. The God of our salvation delights in mercy. When he blots out our transgressions, he does not want us to wallow in the misery of their memory, but to rejoice in his loving-kindness—to do this without delay and to do it unceasingly. Through the prophet Micah, God declared that he would cast our sins into the depths of the sea. It is madness on our part to become deep-sea divers trying to drag them to the surface again! If we have repented and believed the gospel we can leave our sins where God has consigned them—'buried in the sea of God's forgetfulness'. We can celebrate his amazing grace with joy and singing: 'To Him who loves us, and released us from our sins by His blood, and He has made us to be a kingdom, priests to His God and Father; to Him be the glory and the dominion forever and ever' (Rev 1:5–6). This is the joy of salvation and it lays the foundation for a whole life of joy. Many are the joys of the Christian but this excels them all. Above all other blessings we can rejoice that our names are written in heaven. Hallelujah!

The wells of salvation

Speaking of the coming of the Messiah, the prophet Isaiah said, 'In that day you will say: . . . "Surely God is my salvation" . . . with joy you will draw water from the wells of salvation' (Is 12:1–3, NIV). These wells were cisterns, used to store adequate supplies of water, ready for use when needed and leaving their owners without anxiety in the day of drought. The salvation of God provides such wells in abundance and though the land is dry and thirsty we can draw constantly from reservoirs of grace and we can do it with joy. Our salvation begins in the election of God, our names are written in heaven, and one thing is certain—*we* did not write them there. God did it, before the foundation of the world, registering our names in the Lamb's book of life. Our names are recorded there, never to be erased. Jesus expressed it in this way, 'You did not choose Me, but I chose you, and appointed you, that you should go and bear fruit, and that your fruit should remain' (Jn 15:16). In drinking at this well Paul bursts into a paean of praise—'Blessed be the God and Father of our Lord Jesus Christ, who has blessed us with every spiritual blessing . . . in Christ . . . He chose us in Him before the foundation of the world, that we should be holy and blameless before Him' (Eph 1:3–4). This well is very deep but its waters never fail to bring refreshment and joy to those who drink of them. This is why David, in an exuberance of joy, danced before the Lord with all his might (1 Sam 6:14–15): his overflowing joy was rooted in the fact that God had chosen him.

Accepted in Christ

The whole foundation of our salvation is Christ. No other foundation can be laid. Who he is and what he has done in his death and resurrection is the only basis for man to be reconciled to God. And how wonderfully the Lord Jesus has accomplished this! As the innocent Lamb, God laid our sins upon him. He bore our sins in his body on the tree. He answered in full for all our transgressions against God. He has brought us pardon through his blood and life through his death:

> He breaks the power of cancelled sin,
> He sets the prisoner free,
> His blood can make the foulest clean,
> His blood availed for me!
>
> Hear him, ye deaf: His praise, ye dumb,
> Your loosened tongues employ.
> Ye blind, behold your Saviour comes,
> And leap, ye lame, for joy!

But so full is the salvation that God provided in Jesus, it has not only dealt with my sin, transferring it to Christ with all its pollution and appalling consequences, but God has effected a wonderful exchange. *He*, who knew no sin, was made sin for us so that we might experience the righteousness of God. All my demerits were laid on Jesus—all *his* merits are transferred to me. This is truly wonderful—a well of water springing up to eternal life and causing us to sing, 'I will rejoice *greatly* in the Lord, my soul will exult in my God; For He has clothed me with garments of salvation, He has wrapped me with a robe of righteousness' (Is 61:10). Many are the wells of salvation from which we can draw water. They will furnish us with a never-ending supply. The believer need never thirst again and the more he drinks, the more his joy is increased and abounds. This is how one sinner saved expressed it:

> All my soul was dry and dead
> Till I learned that Jesus bled;
> Bled and suffer'd in my place,
> Bearing sin in matchless grace.

Then a drop of Heavenly love
Fell upon me from above,
And by secret, mystic art
Reached the centre of my heart.

Glad the story I recount,
How that drop became a fount,
Bubbled up a living well,
Made my heart begin to swell.

All within my soul was praise,
Praise increasing all my days;
Praise which could not silent be:
Floods were struggling to be free.

More and more the waters grew,
Open wide the flood-gates flew,
Leaping forth in streams of song
Flowed my happy life along.

Lo! a river clear and sweet
Laved my glad, obedient feet!
Soon it rose up to my knees,
And I praised and prayed with ease.

Now my soul in praises swims,
Bathes in songs, and psalms, and hymns;
Plunges down into the deeps,
All her powers in worship steeps.

Hallelujah! O my Lord,
Torrents from my soul are poured!
I am carried clean away,
Praising, praising all the day.

In an ocean of delight,
Praising God with all my might,
Self is drowned. So let it be:
Only Christ remains to me.[5]

C. H. Spurgeon

5

Gladdened by Grace

Barnabas was sent by the church in Jerusalem to see what God was doing among the Gentiles at Antioch. There had been a great stir in the city and God had done the stirring, for the hand of the Lord was with them and a large number who believed turned to the Lord (Acts 11:21). When Barnabas arrived on the scene, that big-hearted man could see clear evidence of the work of God's grace in their lives and he rejoiced or, as the AV puts it: he 'was glad'. It does not really matter which words we use. Gladness and rejoicing are two of a kind and are frequently found together in Scripture. The psalmist says, 'Let all who seek Thee rejoice and be glad in Thee' (Ps 40:16) for truly, grace is a gladdening and transforming thing. All is darkness and gloom until the grace of God appears.

No small wonder then that Barnabas was gladdened to see this life-changing grace evident in the lives of these believers. And wherever grace comes it brings gladness. Any distortion, misunderstanding or blurring of the message of grace has a devastating effect on joy. The message of grace is loud and clear—that salvation in no way depends on us. It is all of grace and it is not of works.

The helplessness of man

By 'works' the Bible means our own homespun righteousness—our religion, our morality, our reputation or anything else that we do or can do. The old covenant was a covenant of works; the awesome command was given 'All the commandments . . . be careful to do that you may live' (Deut 8:1). But though the law is good in the high standard it sets before us, it does not afford us any help to achieve those lofty heights. It puts us well and truly in a state of spiritual tension and frustration. It is like taking a man to Mount Everest and telling him to start climbing but affording him no expertise, no equipment and not even any energy for the task. It is an exercise destined to end in disaster. Man cannot and can never save himself.

The New Testament portrays this graphically, when Paul paints a picture of man's natural condition in black and sombre colours (Eph 2:1–10). The sinner, we learn, is dead in sin and all mankind is shut up in one vast cemetery. This in itself shows up in stark reality the helplessness and hopelessness of man's condition. He can no more save himself than a corpse can, of itself, rise from the grave. Furthermore, mankind is seen here in the grip of an alien power. These evil spiritual forces are at work in society, influencing, moulding and enslaving men.

So from the human standpoint it is a situation of total despair.

The glory of grace

But like a shaft of light breaking through the gloom come these words, 'But God . . . .' And what a God! A God of grace. Not God coming to judge but coming to save. For man's condition is such that only God can save him and that salvation comes by his grace alone. For though man's state is desperate, the grace of God is more than sufficient. For where sin abounded, there grace has much more abounded. This grace, we learn, is a combination of God's almighty power, rich mercy and his intense love, all combined and concentrated to bring the sinner out of his sin, out of the graveyard of guilt and raise him to sit with Christ in heavenly places.

Jesus put the same truth in another way in the parable of the prodigal son. You remember how, after living it up in the far country, squandering all the money his father had given him, and reduced to abject poverty, the son resolved to return with the plea: 'I am no longer worthy to be called your son; make me as one of your hired men.' On returning, he found that his father had other ideas. His father ran to meet him, kissed him again and again, freely forgave him and celebrated his homecoming with a welcome fit for a prince. He deserved none of this and he could never have paid for it all, but it was his father's joy to give it to him. He was glad to have his son back and wanted his son and everyone to share his gladness. That is grace in its essence.

God does not fellowship with us as 'hired men'; we cannot as sinful men and women enter into a business arrangement or commercial contract with God—'I will serve you to make amends for my past failures and to pay for your favour in the future'—he deals with us solely on the grounds of his grace. It is a mercy it is so—for hired men can become fired men if their serving is not up to standard.

The prodigal son was made welcome because he was a son. Even more amazing is the fact that God loved us 'even when we were sinners', for grace lavishes love upon the undeserving.

The homecoming of the youngest son revealed the elder brother's legalistic attitude. Though he had never left his father's household he had never understood his father's heart. He heard the assurance, 'all that is mine is yours'; he did not have to slave for it—it was his already. It was not in his father's heart to withhold anything from him but he failed to realize this. The legalist misunderstands God and misrepresents him. We do not have to slave away to gain his affection. We do not have to coax God to love us. He loves us not because we are lovely or lovable but he loves us, as Charles Wesley put it, 'because He would love'—it is his nature so to do.

The finished work

But we are very reluctant to accept the truth about ourselves. There is within human nature this ingrained error that we can, somehow or other, earn our own salvation or at least contribute in some way toward it. But salvation by grace cancels out all such ideas. Grace focuses our eyes and our hearts upon the merits of the Lord Jesus Christ, the only begotten of the Father, full of grace and truth. It singles him out as the one man who kept the law of God in every respect; who died on the cross not for himself but for us who had transgressed the law and were under its curse and therefore destined to perish eternally. When Jesus died with the shout of victory, 'It is finished' he meant that all we owed had been paid; all that we had failed to do was achieved for us; the curse upon us had been removed. The wages of sin had been meted out to him so that the gift of God might be ours through Jesus Christ our Lord.

So the finished work of Christ is the ground and basis of our eternal salvation and there is no other way. Salvation is by grace through faith and not by works of righteousness that we have done or can do. Any innate desire and tendency to save ourselves or at least to have a share in our salvation must be ruthlessly dealt with. We must

> cast our deadly doing down at Jesus' feet,
> stand in him, in him alone, gloriously complete.

That is terrible poetry but wonderful theology! Its truth was brought home to me on one occasion in a fresh way as I was watching a television programme about Israel. In this particular episode, they were dealing with the custom of the Jewish sabbath and we were shown shoppers in Tel Aviv making their last-minute purchases before the complete cessation of commercial and business life in the city. We were taken inside a typical Israeli home to observe the elaborate preparations for the sabbath. All that was needed to see them through the sabbath period was done— the cleaning, the cooking, the preparations—so that when the candles were lit at sundown on Friday evening nothing more remained to be done. Then came the voice of the commentator in words which went something like this: 'So the housewife, having been busy and caught up in a flurry of activity, now enters into the rest of the sabbath. She has nothing more to do. She can put her feet up and enjoy the sabbath rest.' On hearing that, I recalled how we who believe have 'entered into rest'. The sabbath rest into which we have entered has been prepared not by ourselves or by any others but by the Lord Jesus Christ alone. He has made everything ready. By faith we enter in and enjoy what he has prepared, and we too can 'put our feet up' rejoicing in all the blessings that his death and resurrection have brought us.

The menace of legalism

So far, so good! But it is very important to realize that, having begun in grace, we must continue in grace. It is all too easy to start off well, acknowledging our dependence upon Jesus Christ alone, then reverting to old ways of thinking and behaving, as if everything—or at least something—depended on us. This is what happened to those men and women in Galatia. They started off the Christian race by trusting Christ and then were swerved from their whole-hearted reliance on Jesus alone by teachers who said they needed something more, something additional, such as circumcision and other Jewish religious traditions. This, as Paul points out to them, was completely to change the ground on which they were standing. They had veered from one pathway to another. They had begun on the ground of grace and were now back on the old track of their own works. They were seeking to impose on the work which Christ had done and completed something which emanated from themselves and redounded to their own credit. This was something which could not be done and did not need to be done. In other words, they had become legalists and to be a Christian legalist is a contradiction in terms. We can be truly saved only by grace and Paul was outraged when he heard of the deflection of these believers from the way in which they had first begun by simple trust in the Lord Jesus.

How common it is for believers in our day to fall into the same error and predicament. Endlessly, we endeavour to win or maintain God's favour by some fancied or imagined good in ourselves. Dr J. I. Packer makes a trenchant definition of legalism. He says:

> Legalism means two things: first, supposing that all the law's requirements can be spelled out in a code of standard practice for all situations, a code which

says nothing about the motives, purpose, and spirit of the person acting; second, supposing that formal observance of the code operates in some way as a system of salvation by which we earn our passage to glory or at least gain a degree of divine favour that we would not otherwise enjoy.

He adds:

> The former is . . . decisively exploded by Jesus' insistence that law keeping and law breaking are matters of desire and purpose before ever they become matters of deed and performance. And the latter is destroyed by Paul's gospel of present justification by faith alone, through Christ alone, without works of the law.
>
> Evangelical Christians today are often more successful in avoiding the second facet of legalism than the first. Clear as we are on the formula of forgiveness and acceptance by faith, we make up rules for ourselves and others, beyond what Scripture requires, and treat those who keep them as belonging to a spiritual elite. But this curtailing of personal Christian liberty by group pressure is *not* the way of holiness . . . [the italics are mine].[6]

Neither, we may add, is it the way of joy. To exchange the ground of grace for the treadmill of self-effort is to embark on a never-ending journey that gets you nowhere. All it accomplishes is your own frustration and depression.

Yet we have to confess that legalism is rife among evangelical Christians today. Michelle Guinness has written of her experience as a Jewess who was converted to Christ. What she found among the Christians she met is both informative and alarming. Here are her own devastating words:

> Some Christians had a system of laws more terrible and tyrannical than anything I have ever known as a Jew. A veritable evangelical Torah. The whole lot summed up in one glorious commandment—thou shalt conform.[7]

We may compare it to a person being tried who is acquitted by the judge and so escapes the death penalty. Before the acquitted man has time to sigh with relief, he finds himself serving a life sentence of hard labour, pushed and pressured into a regime of religious rules, regulations and traditions which nullify the word of God.

This is how one lady explained her experience to me:

> Although my middle name is Joy my dad had said he always knew when I had been to a church meeting because I used to come home so miserable. Of course, I had protested but felt annoyed and condemned because I knew he was right. Then one day I heard ministry on 'freedom from law'. I gulped, smiled inanely and tried to forget it. After all, the preacher must be joking, mustn't he! It just didn't fit into my religious upbringing at all. He surely couldn't mean to say that for twenty-three years I had kept all those rules for nothing? Weren't they supposed to make me grow good? Why, apart from the ten commandments there were all the others—no make-up, grow long hair, no dancing, no cinema. I found it really hard to swallow and my husband and I talked to the preacher about it later. He patiently reaffirmed that we were free from law because of Jesus' death and now free to live in the Spirit, and suggested that we read Dr Martyn Lloyd-

Jones on the subject. Quite slowly I realized that I was acceptable to God, that he loved me through and through and that he wanted me to give up my full-time job as a condemnation expert. For me, the truth of being free from law ranks high in bringing about the most radical changes in my life. So began an increasing enjoyment in God, an abandonment in worship, self-acceptance and love of others. It is surprising what can happen when a self-righteous, middle-aged lady is let loose!

Yes, all too easily we can impose upon the gospel of God's free grace man-made conditions and traditions. The young Christian in his first flush of joy in finding salvation in Christ is all too frequently instructed by well-meaning people who impress upon him a lifestyle that they think is just what a young Christian needs. In that way we are given a whole load of human tradition, rules and regulations to guide us and then we quickly discover that what was given to guide us has become our chain. A lot of preaching is simply demanding the impossible, setting out the task before the people without providing the means. In other words, our preaching is an inducement to self-effort, presenting what we are pleased to call 'the challenge' of the Christian life, bombarding people with an endless flow of exhortations to witness, to serve, to read the Bible every day and to pray regularly—all very worthy ends in themselves but presented so as to burden them rather than inspire them.

Now let it be said that no faithful preacher of the word will fail to urge Christians to work out their own salvation with fear and trembling, but he must always keep before him and his hearers the astounding truth that this may only be attempted—and certainly can only be achieved—on the basis of the fact that 'God is at work in you'. The mighty God is at work in us, to accomplish his good pleasure. Merely to tell people to work out their own salvation is like telling a man to fly. But to tell him that God is at work in him, to accomplish his purpose, will give him wings.

Living in grace

All our efforts must flow from divine energizing and not from our own strength. As Paul put it in his letter to the Colossians, 'I labor, striving according to his power which mightily works within me' (Col 1:29). In writing to the Galatians, Paul uses the old story of the two children of Abraham as an allegory. You will recall that Sarah had persuaded Abraham to have a child by his slave-girl, Hagar, so Hagar became a surrogate mother (there is nothing new under the sun, but notice that this situation brought many problems then as it does now). So Ishmael was born. But God's purpose was that Sarah herself should have a son. At a time when it was physically impossible for her and Abraham to have children, God wrought a miracle and Isaac was born.

Taking up these historical facts, Paul develops his allegory. The two women represent two covenants—one, a covenant of works, which is slavery; the other, a covenant of grace, which is liberty. Hagar's child was born of the energy and impulse of the flesh. Sarah's son was born according to the Spirit. The two elements represented by these two sons cannot co-exist and live together. The son of the bond-woman had to be cast out and, though Ishmael had been there a good many years, on God's command he went. The casting out of legalism with its bondage and misery from our lives and churches is long overdue. It is a work of the flesh and we, as believers, are children of the Spirit, children of liberty and children of joy. So Paul concludes the allegory with the call to rejoice—'Rejoice, barren woman who does not bear; break forth and shout, you who are not in labor; for more are the children of the desolate than of the one who has a husband' (Gal 4:27).

If you are not living in the joy of the Lord, look and see whether you are not living under God in the energy of the flesh, by self-effort, seeking by your own strength either to win or to maintain God's favour, and cast out that attitude and behaviour and live in grace and upon grace. God begins with us where we are when we have nothing to commend ourselves. That is always true of us. All our enrichment, all our enabling is in Christ and in him alone. That is the ground of grace and it is liberating and it is that which gladdens the heart of man.

Fall into grace

If we are concerned to live a life of joy we must take care not to fall from grace. To take the retrograde step of embracing a 'do-it-yourself' salvation is both foolish and futile. For Scripture declares, 'By the works of the Law, shall no flesh be justified' (Gal 2:16). It is a dead-end that leads to despair. Rather, let us fall more and more *into* grace, which rejoices in the free, undeserved gift of God. The Christian believer does not have to work to obtain eternal life. He has it as a gift of God's grace. He does not seek to live a holy life to become a saint—the grace of God has made him a saint and enables him to live in a saintly way. This will sustain him in joy. Whenever the believer is tempted to sin this grace will shout in his ear, 'God forbid!'. This grace will activate the believer to fight, oppose and conquer sin wherever sin has conquered him. This grace will teach the believer to deny ungodliness and worldly desire, to live sensibly, righteously and godly in this present age. This grace will assure the believer that God will finish the work he has begun. He will not tire of us or weary of our failures and weaknesses, but will persevere until in the end we are conformed to the image of his Son. As John Newton observes:

> Through many dangers, snares and fears,
> I have already come:
> 'Twas grace that brought me safe thus far,
> And grace will lead me home.

6

Expressing Our Joy

Preaching on one occasion on the need to rejoice evermore, I was approached by a lady after the service who assured me, 'We do rejoice here but we don't show it.' Then, before I could comment on this, she added, 'After all, we *are* English.'

Yes, culture does get in the way of our doing God's will at times. Many of us are learning that all culture—English or whatever nationality— must be adjusted to the culture of the kingdom of God. I was able to assure this good woman that the God who saved me from my sins could save me from my Englishness. I think it would be a task bordering on the impossible for anyone to express joy unspeakable and full of glory with the British stiff upper lip!

When Peter and John showed the power of the name of Jesus by healing the lame man who was begging at the temple gate, that man had such a mighty infusion of the power of God that he was walking, leaping and praising God. In vain you would have sent some dignified deacon to tell him not to be so exuberant. He had known the self-same power that raised Jesus from the dead pulsating through his body. His joy knew no bounds and without asking anyone's permission he gave free expression to it.

Expressing our emotions

In suppressing our emotions we fly in the face of our creator's wisdom. He has made us so that laughter and tears are a God-given safety valve that release us from the tensions of life. In saying this, we are not in any way advocating emotionalism; but in our fear of emotion we have swung to the other extreme of ignoring our emotional nature and needs altogether. What we are pleading for is that God-given emotions be given their rightful place in our worship, controlled by the Spirit of God. It is nothing short of ridiculous that when we come together to worship we dehumanize ourselves by leaving, as it were, our emotions at home, determining to hide all our inner feelings behind a mask of unbiblical religiosity. We have become so hidebound in our religious traditions that we are like Lazarus—out of the grave but bound hand and foot by the grave-clothes. There is as much emotion and movement as you would find in an Egyptian mummy!

F. D. Bruner in his book *A Theology of the Holy Spirit* says: 'The Pentecostal often asks why joy and its expression should be permitted in almost every kind of human convocation except the church.'[8] Why, indeed? We express our emotions without reserve in other areas of life and living. Go to any sports stadium or centre where the crowds gather to cheer their favourite teams, whether it be soccer, rugby or swimming: the air is filled with shouting, clapping and singing—often borrowing our hymn tunes! They are wholly caught up in the excitement of the game. Even the more refined and genteel sports have their enthusiasts. Of one eminent spectator it has been written: 'She can forget her position sufficiently to leap up and down like any enthusiast, shouting and waving.' The lady referred to is Her Majesty Queen Elizabeth II. The writer adds: 'When her horse has won, you see reborn the delighted monkey grin of childhood photos.'[9]

Often in these situations, all the excitement is generated because a ball filled with air is being passed from player to player and headed into the goal; or else a horse has passed the post. What better and greater reasons have the redeemed of the Lord to rejoice and to show their rejoicing—to clap, to sing, to shout, to leap up and down—when they celebrate together the mighty acts of God. Why should we hold back any part of our being in bringing our worship to God? Let all that is within us be stirred to bless his holy name. Our spirits, our souls, our bodies, our minds, our feelings, our intellects, our emotions—let all unite to celebrate his praise.

The book of Psalms was the ancient hymn-book of Israel and we know that the psalms formed an integral and important part of the worship of the early church (Eph 5:19). And the psalms not only incite and encourage us to praise the Lord but show us how to do it. These worshippers praised God with a verve and vitality that demanded all their powers. It was truly a sacrifice of praise: they did not offer something to the Lord which cost them nothing. All their powers were given full range—body, soul, spirit, mind, emotions and will—all were concerted and co-ordinated to praise the God of our salvation. For instance, their worship was vibrant with music. There was the sound of trumpets and of the crashing cymbals and many other instruments. Their worship was characterized by movement. There were clapping hands and dancing feet which gave expression to their incredible joy in God. Their worship was also vocal with singing and shouting, cries of 'Hosanna' and 'Hallelujah'. For when the Bible tells us to make a joyful noise to the Lord it does not mean that we have a licence to sing a hymn badly or murder a good melody with raucous sounds. It means just what it says—making a noise to the Lord from a heart full of joy. When Christ rode into Jerusalem on the wild colt of an ass, the multitudes of disciples began to praise God joyfully with a loud voice. They did this by shouting out 'Blessed is he who comes in the name of the Lord! . . . Hosanna in the highest!' This kind of worship was frowned upon by the Pharisees but accepted and approved by the Lord Jesus. For the only thing that concerns true worshippers is 'What does the Lord want? What pleases *him*?' David's wife, Michal, disapproved strongly of her husband's dancing because she thought it demeaned him in the eyes of others. But that praising, joyful, worshipping man had eyes and heart for God alone. He swept all her objections aside saying, 'It was before the *Lord*' that I did it.

Many have discovered in their own church fellowships that one of the things the Spirit of God is doing among the churches is releasing us into spontaneous praise and exuberant joy. This has made for a radical change in the pattern of our worship. Instead of one predominant pipe organ, there are now many players on a variety of instruments. There is singing, but there is also shouting. There is dancing with exuberant joy. Sometimes there is kneeling and prostration before the awesome presence of God. There are prophetic utterances and prophetic songs. There is spontaneous applause as we recount together the wonderful works of God, and even more applause if we *see* the wonderful works of God. Many of us would have been shocked to be present at some of the meetings that Jesus attended when, during a synagogue service, demon-possessed people screamed out; or when the liturgy of the synagogue was brought to a halt as he ordered a man with a withered hand to stretch it out; or when, in a house-meeting one day as he was speaking, clods of clay and dust and dirt fell on the people listening to his teaching. What a commotion that must have made, for someone was breaking up the roof and lowering a man on a stretcher through the hole. But the Lord Jesus was quite unperturbed about all this. He cares nothing for our obsession with dignity and our misunderstanding of the verse which says that everything 'should be done decently and in order' (1 Cor 14:40). Divine disturbance was the order of the

day. The man on the stretcher found forgiveness
of sin and healing for his body, and God was
glorified.

Dr J. I. Packer has some valuable words to say
in his book *Keep in step with the Spirit* on this very
theme. He says:

There is a subtle tenacity abroad that remains
wedded to the way things were done a hundred
years ago. It thinks that it renders God service by
being *faithful* (that is the word used) to these out-
moded fashions; it never faces the possibility that
they might need amending today if ever we are to
communicate effectively with each other and with
those outside our circle. Letting our inherited build-
ings dictate what we do and do not do when we meet
in them is part of this traditionalist syndrome—and
is often a very potent part, as surely we can all see.
Churches tend to run in grooves of conventionality,
and such grooves quickly turn into graves.

Here is where the challenge to institutional rad-
icalism comes in: a challenge to which charismatic
groups have been noticeably more alert than some
others. Only styles and structures that serve the
Spirit should stand. Everything bogging us down in
lifeless routine or restraining the fruitful use of
spiritual gifts or encouraging the people in the pews
to become passengers should be changed, no matter
how sacrosanct we previously took it to be. The Holy
Spirit is not a sentimentalist as too many of us are;
he is a change agent, and he comes to change
human structures as well as human hearts. Change
for its own sake is mere fidgeting, but change that
gets rid of obstacles to God's fullest blessing is both a
necessity and a mercy.[10]

It would be fitting at this point to quote again

from the writings of C. H. Spurgeon commenting on Psalm 149:3—'Let them praise His name with dancing; let them sing praises to Him with timbrel and lyre.' He writes:

Thus let them repeat the triumph of the Red Sea which was ever the typical glory of Israel. Miriam led the daughters of Israel in the dance when the Lord had triumphed gloriously; was it not most fit that she should? The sacred dance of devout joy is no example, nor even excuse, for frivolous dances, much less for lewd ones. Who could help dancing when Egypt was vanquished, and the tribes were free? Every mode of expressing delight was bound to be employed on so memorable occasion. Dancing, singing, and playing on instruments were all called into requisition, and most fitly so. There are unusual seasons which call for unusual expressions of joy. When the Lord saves a soul its holy joy overflows, and it cannot find channels enough for its exceeding gratitude: if the man does not leap, or play, or sing, at any rate he praises God, and wishes for a thousand tongues with which to magnify his Saviour. Who would wish it to be otherwise? Young converts are not to be restrained in their joy. Let them sing and dance while they can. How can they mourn now that their Bridegroom is with them? Let us give the utmost liberty to joy. Let us never attempt its suppression, but issue in the terms of this verse a double license for exultation. If any ought to be glad it is the children of Zion; rejoicing is more fit for Israel than for any other people: it is their own folly and fault that they are not oftener brimming with joy in God, for the very thought of him is delight.[11]

Only one thing needs to be added. Let us make sure that we get things in the right order. We do not sing, clap and dance to bring ourselves into joyful praise. We are not using these to work things up and bring us into joy. Neither do we want to indulge in a preliminary singalong to fit us for worship. This, in my view, is fatal. No, the truth of the matter is that we must come together filled with the Spirit, filled with joy, actually entering his courts with thanksgiving and his gates with praise—then, brimming over with joy, give the fullest expression to it.

7

The Joy of Prayer

Prayer and joy. What a strange combination! Many people would never associate the two and would fail to see the remotest connection between them. But Jesus has joined them together—'Ask, and you will receive, that your joy may be made full' (Jn 16:24). For many, prayer is just a religious exercise. It is sombre and dull, a routine from which all delight has been drained away. It has become for them a burden and almost a drudge. For others it is nothing more than a problem area. How enlivening and exciting then are these words of Jesus, 'Ask . . . that your joy may be made full.' Could we but believe the great and magnificent promises God has given in regard to prayer we should never again look upon it as a religious chore but rather as one of the most exhilarating enterprises we could ever engage in. To come before God with specific needs: to ask, to seek and to knock and then to prove for ourselves the words of Jesus, 'It *shall* be given to you' (Mt

7:7), strengthens your faith, inflames your love and fills the heart with joy.

In one of the churches I served as pastor we came into contact with a little lady who remained very much on the fringe of the fellowship. She lived in a tiny apartment and gave every appearance of not possessing much of this world's goods. We did not see a lot of her in the church gatherings but she always appeared when we were providing meals. Altogether she gave the impression of eking out a frugal existence on a very low income. Some years later she died, and imagine our amazement when, after her death, her will was published in the national press. She had left (alas, not to me!) a sum of thousands of pounds, which in those days was a small fortune. She had been a very rich woman but she preferred for some strange reason to live near the poverty line.

Many of us emulate her in this sense. We are wealthy beyond words, rich with all the riches of God's promises and yet we are content to live as though we were on the breadline or did not have them. We live on a poverty-stricken pittance when we could be living like kings. This is madness—to deprive ourselves and the church of Christ of that which our risen Head longs to give to us. Jesus himself has given us that golden promise, 'Whatever you ask in My name, that will I do, that the Father may be glorified in the Son. If you ask Me anything in My name, I will do it' (Jn 14:13–14).

As we look at those words we can rejoice in the scope of his promise. Whatever and anything. These words are very wide in their comprehensiveness. They could not be wider! So don't let us devalue them or underrate them in any way but let them stand and let them stimulate faith in our hearts. *Whatever* or *anything*. Repeat the words to yourself again and again. Whatever we need, anything we ask. Don't minimize them or put limitations upon them. If we will take them as they stand they will quicken a living faith that the things which are impossible with men *are* possible with God. When you see this promise you can say with Charles Wesley:

> Faith, mighty faith, the promise sees
> And looks to that alone:
> Laughs at impossibilities
> And cries 'It shall be done.'

Armed with such a promise we shall not come to a halt in these evil days or call a retreat. We shall not be daunted by any crisis or frightened by the facts. However frightening the facts may be, we know that God is greater so the crisis is cut down to proper proportions before the might and majesty of our God. So let these words 'whatever' and 'anything' be to you the joy and rejoicing of your heart. They proclaim the wonderful truth that with God all things are possible.

Also, we can rejoice in the certainty that prayer will be answered. What joy comes when God acts according to our asking. We prove the promise for ourselves. We actually receive what we have asked of him and, as we receive, we know a fresh influx of joy.

Hannah was desperate for a child. She prayed to God with strong crying, tears and vows. Eli the priest misjudged her, thinking for the moment that she was intoxicated with wine, but Hannah assured him that in her continual praying she had poured out her soul before the Lord. (What a description of true prayer that is!) Soon, Eli was saying to her, 'Go in peace; and may the God of Israel grant your petition that you have asked of Him' (1 Sam 1:17). Then we see a dramatic change in Hannah. She was no longer sad. Her grief had gone. The words brought her assurance that God had heard her prayer and the answer was on the way. She knew joy instead of sorrow once that assurance was given, then more joy when her son was actually born. Her joyful heart overflowed in song: 'My soul exults in the Lord . . . I rejoice in Thy salvation' (1 Sam 2:1).

I remember so vividly in the early days of our church in Hove that we were meeting in a local school and very quickly filled the gymnasium, which was the largest hall in the building. Our need to find premises of our own became urgent and it was our custom as elders to meet on Thursday mornings to wait on God and to bring before him the needs of his people. On one of these mornings we were burdened to ask the Lord for a building of our own. It was an amazing time! As we prayed, God enlarged our faith and desire; we were enabled to lay hold of God. He spoke to us in a word of prophecy: 'Trust me like little children, who naively ask their parents what they want, never for one moment considering how or where it can be obtained.' Then simultaneously as we continued praying, each of us had the assurance in our heart that our request had been granted. Without any prompting, we burst into praise and jubilation. We *knew* that something had been settled. It was just a matter of time before we actually experienced God's provision; within a few days, we received a telephone call 'out of the blue' that marked the beginning of negotiations that enabled us to occupy our present premises within a few months. It was a gift from God, given in direct answer to prayer. This is but one example of the many that could be given. I am convinced that the man or the church that makes it their habitual practice to bring specific needs to God in faith, proving continually the generosity of his heart, will know more and more of glorious joy as they receive the answer to their prayers.

Above all, we can rejoice in the One who sent this word and gave us this promise—the Lord Jesus Christ—and it is in his name that we can ask. Through his name we can approach God. We do not and never will have anything in ourselves that gives us the right to come to God and ask anything of him. But the Lord Jesus, by his atoning death and resurrection has made a way into the presence of God for us. It is a newly slain and living way which he has consecrated by his blood; we may come to our holy God and come confidently. We need not keep away for any reason. The throne of grace is the place where we can obtain mercy and grace to help in time of need.

When serving the Lord in India, my companion and I planned to visit the believers in Nepal. Richard and I took a plane to New Delhi, only to discover that the seats we had reserved on the plane to Katmandu were already taken. This we were to discover was not an unusual occurrence, but it presented us with a major problem. Our time was very restricted and it was essential that we arrive in Nepal that day in order to take the internal connecting flight that had been arranged and so reach our final destination. We were assured it was most unlikely that we would get a flight that day. So New Delhi airport became a place of prayer.

After some time God marvellously answered our prayer by giving us favour with an Indian official who obtained seats for us on another airline, and some hours later we arrived in Katmandu. The brother due to meet us had left the airport—resulting in our offering more prayer and strong crying to God. When he eventually arrived, we learned that we had missed our internal flight. We would have to stay the night in Katmandu and try again the next day.

Early the next morning we checked in at the airport. Our luggage was taken and we thought we were about to depart but, no, there was a notice of delay and time was passing—one hour, two hours, three hours—and then our luggage was returned to us with the drastic news that all flights had been cancelled!

So once again we were cast utterly upon God and we cried to him. Tell us, Lord, what to do! Should we ask him for wings? But we decided that the air in the Himalayas would be a little too chilly for us. Peter, the brother who had met us, had already been looking at the possibility of travelling by road if we could hire a taxi. But wherever he went to enquire, none seemed to be available. We continued to pray and as we prayed I felt God say at one point: 'Take a taxi.' And though I knew that Peter had already tried to do this and failed, I heard myself saying to him, 'Go and get a taxi!' I was surprised at the authority with which I was able to speak and also at the alacrity with which Peter moved. Though he had been many times without success, he now immediately disappeared into the bustling city. Some half an hour later he returned triumphantly, saying that he had arranged a taxi to take us all the way. 'All the way' meant a six-hour journey along mountainous roads which can best be described as bumpy, very bumpy and very very bumpy. Also, we discovered that the taxi was a mini-bus and, instead of four persons including the driver, we were a party of fifteen. We arrived late at night, bruised and weary but filled with joy. God had answered our prayers and we were able to fulfil our planned meetings and with joy serve the believers in Nepal.

Getting back to the scope of Jesus' promise, let us realize that to ask in his name means that we are abiding in him—that he is our life, our strength; that we allow him to shape our desires so that our prayers are coloured and controlled by his will and his purpose. To ask in the name of Jesus does not mean that you tag the name of Jesus on to the end of your prayer to cover up all your self-will, self-love and selfish motives. It is not that at all. It means that you are so joined to Christ that the desires of his heart have become your desires too. That is why this word is reserved for those who are abiding in Christ. For if you were to say to the average man, 'Have what you will!', his reply would probably be for a new car or a marvellous physique or a win on the football pools and such a rich promise would be squandered on trivial and transient pleasures. Even many believers cannot be trusted with a word like this because there is so much 'self' in them. As James 4:3 clearly states, they would be asking from the wrong motives. In verse 2 James is very positive, 'You do not have because you do not ask.' Then to those who have asked, he continues, 'You ask and do not receive, because you ask with wrong motives, so that you may spend it on your pleasures.' If we are asking in that kind of way, James tells us that we shall not receive it. We have to have our motives cleansed and purified. We have to be people who are 'in God' and desire his will above everything.

This reminds us again of the priorities of the Lord Jesus when he taught us about prayer, saying, 'Our Father who art in heaven, hallowed be Thy name; Thy kingdom come. Thy will be done, on earth, as it is in heaven' (Mt 6:9–10).

Notice that it begins with God. It is all about God. It is taken up with God as are all great prayers. One of the reasons why our prayers are not answered is that we haven't really lost our hearts, lost our wills and lost ourselves utterly in God and what he wants. We are asking with wrong motives and we do not receive because God will never pander to our selfishness. But if we abide in Jesus, we shall ask what we will and it shall be done and the word of the Lord is that our joy will be full.

We must not overlook the implications of this word. What Christ is saying here clearly implies that our joylessness is tied up with our prayerlessness. Let us see that we are men and women of prayer so that, receiving from God that which we ask, our joy will be full. And it will be *kept* full as we make it our habitual practice to keep appearing before God with a believing heart and empty hands and then to come away laden with the blessings of heaven—to know by our daily experience that God is a rewarder of those who diligently seek him. All this is a sure way to be kept in fullness of joy.

Let us also realize that although it is good to pray as individuals, joy can be multiplied when we pray corporately. To seek God together, to ask in the name of Jesus together, will mean that we shall rejoice together when, in answer to prayer, we see the needed finances come in, souls saved or the devil routed. There will surely be a fresh anointing of joy upon the praying assembly. The prayer meeting will become aglow with the praise of God and you do not have to urge people to attend meetings like that. No, on the contrary— you can't keep them away! For they become pure, unadulterated joy—a joy to attend, a joy to ask, a joy to receive—it is joy, joy, joy. Just as Jesus said, ask that your joy may be full.

8

Joy and Delight in the Word

Another source of joy the Holy Spirit uses is the written word of God. He wants us to share the experience of the psalmist who said, 'I rejoice at Thy word, as one who finds great spoil' (Ps 119: 162). What a wonderful combination of treasure and pleasure! But it is sometimes a very different story that believers have to relate in their Bible reading.

During the First World War of 1914–18 (I am reliably informed) there appeared posters showing a portrait of a bewhiskered General Kitchener pointing his finger at all and sundry saying, 'Your country needs you!' I remember in the days of my youth looking upon another poster, not unlike those recruiting posters, portraying a black-suited man with a solemn religious expression pointing to a black leather-bound Bible with the caption underneath, 'Have you read your Bible today?' Its purpose was to encourage people to do this, but for me it was all too self-defeating—the question was loaded with legal obligation and the poster was shrouded in religious gloom and bereft of any hint that our Bible reading could be pleasant as well as profitable.

There is no doubt as to the benefits of regular reading of the Bible, but all too frequently it has been presented in a heavy-handed fashion, laid down as our bounden duty rather than set before us as something delightful and desirable. This is a great pity, and no Christian should rest content until he is able truthfully to say with Jeremiah, 'Thy words were found and I ate them, and Thy words became for me a joy and the delight of my heart' (Jer 15:16). If our reading of the word of God has not been like that, do believe that it can be and ask God to make it so for you—a joy and a delight. You wouldn't want to miss that, would you? And God does not want you to miss it either.

Let me share with you now some of the ways in which God has brought joy to me through the word. First of all, read it regularly. Every day. But don't limit yourself to that. Have a special set time, but don't get locked in to a special time— make other opportunities to dip into its truth. I remember how the pastor of the Baptist church where I was brought up—a true man of God and a man of the word—carried with him a pocket Bible. He would seize opportunities to read a few verses here and there. If he was travelling, he would dip into the word on the journey. If he had an appointment and was kept waiting, he would take out the Bible and read some portion whilst waiting. Truly, it is quite astounding to discover how many hours can be retrieved from utter loss and filled with fresh light and joy through the word, when we use these moments in this way. We are spoilt for choice in the West, when it comes to the availability of Scripture, so we can have Bibles in various versions in all sorts of places scattered around the home so that, as the opportunity presents itself, we can, as it were, take a snack and feed on the word of God for a few moments.

In the special time that I set aside to read the word of God, I have found it very valuable to read the word *slowly*. It is very easy to rush on in reading, our eyes skimming the words but not exploring to the full the truth they convey. Much good is lost in this way. As a quick reader, I find it helpful to write out the Scriptures. This slows me down considerably—it makes me lie down in green pastures instead of barging my way through them without feeding upon them. So much revelation comes, I find, from writing the word of God.

Another method is to listen to the word of God being read. Tape cassettes of the Bible are widely available now. I find it an enormous stimulus to hear the Bible read audibly by a reader who can articulate the words naturally and clearly (not in parsonic tones, please)—a reader who is mindful of punctuation marks and can inflect his voice to bring the needed emphasis.

But whether we listen to, write or read the word, the important thing is that we hear God speaking to us through the word. This is a crucial point. So much Bible study has become an academic exercise. It is stamped with the ethos of the college and classroom when it should be an audience with a reconciled God, the beloved reading the love-letters of her Lover—a whole stimulus to greater love and zeal for the Lord our God. It is very proper that, when we come to the word, we should come with the prayer of Samuel—'Speak, Lord, for Thy servant is listening' (1 Sam 3:9). For Jeremiah, the words God actually spoke to him became the written word, enshrined for ever in our Bible. For us, the written word is that which God uses to speak words to us fitting to our need, tailored to our circumstances, ministering love and consolation and joy to our hearts. To hear God speak through his word is joy indeed—as Charles Wesley describes it so perfectly:

> Oh, that I could for ever sit
> With Mary at the Master's feet;
> Be this my happy choice,
> My only care, delight and bliss,
> My joy, my heaven on earth be this,
> To hear the Bridegroom's voice.

Another essential to joyful Bible reading is to understand it. When the eunuch sat in his chariot reading the book of the prophet Isaiah, Philip asked him, 'Do you understand what you are reading?' Good question! I think it should be asked more often. It was the Spirit who led Philip to this man by supernatural direction. It was the Spirit who said to Philip: 'Go up and join this chariot.' But notice that the Spirit was not satisfied with the eunuch merely reading the Bible—he wanted him to understand. And for this reason he sent Philip to make clear to the eunuch the truth of God. Let us not debunk the God-given faculty of human reasoning. The Spirit never bypasses our minds, though he often transcends them. He honours the human mind, darkened though it is, and seeks to bring it to an understanding of the gospel. As we note here that he did this through Philip, so we should be thankful for ministries set in the church by the ascended Christ—evangelists who make the message clear and plain; for teachers past and present who labour to bring us into an even greater understanding of the truth.

Joy will arise as we appropriate the word; that is, as we apply it to ourselves. When we see our personal interest is involved, it will hold our attention. If you are present at the reading of a will, it will not capture your interest with its legal terminology, its convoluted phrases, its repetitions of legal jargon. But if the will has your name written down and a legacy has been left to you, suddenly what has been a tedious or even a boring exercise takes on a more delightful dimension. The mention of your name and the prospect of coming wealth will wonderfully concentrate and uplift your mind. So when you read the word remember that you are a beneficiary. It is a testament to reveal to you the spoil and the treasure that has come to you in Christ. By God's grace you are an heir of God and a joint heir with Christ, and all the promises of God receive their 'yes' and 'amen' in him. As you read words such as 'I live by faith in the Son of God, who loved me, and delivered Himself up for me' (Gal 2:20), let your heart and mind linger on the word 'me'. He loved *me* and gave himself for *me*. The personal application of the word to your own heart, need and condition will marvellously contribute to your growth in grace and the knowledge of our Lord Jesus Christ.

As we read let us also assimilate the word. Jeremiah said, 'Thy words were found and I ate them.' That is how we should hear the word of life, remembering that 'man shall not live by bread alone, but on every word that proceeds out of the mouth of God' (Mt 4:4). These words of Jesus are Spirit and life. They can create, sustain and strengthen life and so I need to feed on the word. The word is set forth in the Scripture as my necessary food. Peter urges new Christians, '. . . like newborn babes, long for the pure milk of the word, that by it you may grow in respect to salvation, if you have tasted the kindness of the Lord' (1 Pet 2:2–3).

All who believe have been saved by the Spirit of God using some word of Scripture that revealed to them the Lord Jesus. That initial receiving of the word was but a taste ('sweeter than honey', as the psalmist described it) that should have whetted our appetites to hunger to know more of the Lord as he is revealed in all the Scriptures.

Let us then read, mark, learn and inwardly digest, feeding our spiritual lives upon the word of God. Having tasted, let us partake to the full of the feast that God has provided for us in the Scripture.

Then, we must meditate—that is, treasure the word, turn it over again and again in our minds. As a sheep will eat grass and chew the cud, so let us recall and ruminate in our minds upon the truth of God, extracting all the goodness and nourishment that we can find. It is an excellent idea to read some verses again and again, to recall them as you go through the day. For the advantage of meditation is that you can meditate whilst you are doing other things—when you are mowing the lawn, driving the car or preparing a meal. Many are the blessings of meditation and among them is this—that it is a delightful thing. Psalm 1 says, 'How blessed is the man who does not walk in the counsel of the wicked . . . his delight is in the law of the Lord, and in His law he meditates day and night and he will be like a tree firmly planted by streams of water, which yields its fruit in its season, and its leaf does not wither; and in whatever he does, he prospers.' Notice he makes mention of day and night. For the night-time may not only be spent in sleep—it can be bright with the visitation of God as you meditate upon the word.

Another element in finding joy in the word is to memorize it. How thankful I am that as a child I was taught to learn the Scriptures by heart. Badgered and bribed, I learnt whole chunks of God's word, not really appreciating its value at the time, but it has proved to be a treasury throughout life. I believe it to be true to say that committing the Scriptures to memory is not so common today as it once was. This is perhaps largely because modern educational methods decry the value of learning by rote and also because there are so many versions of the Bible that there is no longer the standard criterion of the Authorized Version, which reigned supreme in my day. There is, however, a compensating factor today in that many scripture passages are now set to melodies that make it easy for us to memorize them. As we sing them with others in our worship time, the Scriptures become stored in our hearts and in our minds. This can only be to our great good. The blessings and benefits that have come to me in my life and ministry through the memorized Scriptures are incalculable. It is a wonderful thing to be able to turn out the light, close my eyes and then, with my own inbuilt overhead projector in my mind, project the word of God before me —some psalm, some chapter of scripture. I find that I am remembering, reading, meditating and rejoicing in the truth—which leads me to say this: we must pray over the word and pray it *into* our lives. In fact, you can turn what you read into prayer. Our private times with God were never meant to be monologues but a dialogue. When the psalmist heard God say to him, 'Seek my face,' *he* said to the Lord, 'Thy face, O Lord, I shall seek' (Ps 27:8). This is the way to fellowship with God and prolong our times before him. As we read the word we embrace the promises, we get enthralled by the prophecies and are enabled to pray for their fulfilment, we obtain grace to put into practice the various precepts, and all the way through we can pray over the word of God.

The end of our hearing is to obey. Jesus said that to hear his word and to do it means that we put a firm, solid foundation into our lives which will stand the test of time and eternity, whatever storms may arise. And it must be said that the massive spiritual snarl-ups in our lives can frequently be traced back not so much to failing to read our Bibles but to not doing what the Lord asked us to do. All too often we are like the man of whom the apostle James speaks, who looks at his face in the mirror then puts it down in a great hurry to forget what he has seen. But, says the apostle, 'One who looks intently at the perfect law, the law of liberty, and abides by it, not having become a forgetful hearer but an effectual doer, this man shall be blessed in what he does' (Jas 1:25). Or as Jesus put it, 'If you know these things, you are blessed if you do them' (Jn 13:17).

Just one more thing remains to be said about the word and the joy it affords to us—that is we are called to share it. As Christians we are called to 'hold out the word of life' (Phil 2:16, NIV). Let us be like the sower in the parable who went forth to sow. The seed he sowed was the word of God. Likewise, let us scatter it everywhere and all the time. This will bring us a lot of labour but, in the end, terrific joy. 'Those who sow with tears shall reap with joyful shouting. He who goes to and fro weeping, carrying his bag of seed, shall indeed come again with a shout of joy, bringing his sheaves with him' (Ps 126:5–6).

Many are the joys that Scripture affords us. Its words make us wise unto salvation, they are a safeguard against sin and that will keep us in joy. They are divinely inspired and profitable for us as they teach, reprove, correct and train us in righteousness. They are the comprehensive equipment for the man of God. But, above all other joys, the Bible is full of Christ—it speaks of him. Jesus himself says: 'It is these [the Scriptures] that bear witness of Me' (Jn 5:39). The distinguishing glory of the Bible is that in reading the written word we meet with the living Word, and to meet with Jesus is joy unspeakable.

9

Joy in Serving

Believers in Christ are blessed with every spiritual blessing in him, and among those blessings is the call to share in his mission. In mercy he makes use of us. So all those saved by the Lord are called to be the servants of the Lord. This is an honour we share with the angels, who were created and exist solely to do his pleasure. We were created and redeemed to serve our God for ever.

Such service is not to be thought of as certain 'Christian activities' but rather a total devotion of our whole lives to God, affecting all areas of daily life and living. Serving the Lord in the Bible means living life unto God and for his glory. To be a co-worker with God and a fellow servant with Christ is an unspeakable privilege that should fill our hearts with continual joy. Gratitude to God for salvation should motivate us to serve him. The believer is one who instinctively keeps asking, 'What shall I render unto the Lord for all his benefits to me?' And we should begin every day, as Paul began his Christian life, with the prayer, 'What shall I do, Lord?' (Acts 22:10).

Serving with gladness

But our calling is not only to serve the Lord; we are to do it with joy. Why should we seek to serve him in any other way? It affords the greatest delight to serve the King of kings. It should be our supreme pleasure to do his will and run in the way of his commandments. For he is no hard Pharaoh who makes us serve with rigour, but our Saviour and Master who counts his servants his friends and his friends his servants. If he has a yoke, it is easy; if he has a burden, it is light. We dishonour him when we regard his service as something to be done only with reluctance or to be avoided if we can—likewise, when we present his will as something disagreeable rather than good, perfect and acceptable. For his will is not to be regarded as a great calamity but welcomed as the greatest blessing that we can know.

Israel was warned: 'Because you did not serve the Lord your God with joy and a glad heart, for the abundance of all things; therefore you shall serve your enemies . . .' (Deut 28:47). It is no light thing, then, to cast a slur upon God's character by seeking to serve him in a sullen or morose spirit. Rather let us with exceeding joy be 'always abounding in the work of the Lord' (1 Cor 15:58).

Frances Ridley Havergal was the writer of many lovely hymns and probably the best known and loved is 'Take my life and let it be, consecrated, Lord, to Thee.' It is truly a great hymn but has suffered and I think lost some of its spiritual impact by being wedded to melodies extremely funereal in tone. It is a hymn that cries aloud to be matched to a tune vibrant with the joy of the Lord and suffused with hallelujahs. Why should we approach God's service in deep mourning or gather for worship like an assembly of undertakers? Let us, as children of the heavenly King, spread our joys abroad and celebrate his astonishing grace in calling us to be his servants.

The example of the Lord Jesus

Jesus was a man of joy and he was pre-eminently a servant. God speaks of him in the prophetic Scriptures, 'Behold, My Servant, who I uphold; My chosen one in whom My soul delights. I have put My Spirit upon Him' (Is 42:1). The New Testament quotes this verse to describe the ministry of the Lord Jesus, and he himself said, 'The Son of Man did not come to be served, but to serve, and to give His life a ransom for many' (Mt 20:28). His whole life and death were a demonstration of joyful dedication to the will of God and of service to others.

Those who have found joy in God instinctively share it with others, for joy does not thrive in the soil of selfishness. Selfish people will never be truly happy. Christ, we are told, 'pleased not himself', and to be free of selfishness is the royal road to joy. Many who are weighed down by their own concerns and problems would find their load lightened if they became interested and involved in the lives of others. To mope and dwell upon our own needs is a sure recipe for depression but to reach out to others and genuinely seek their welfare, fulfilling the law of Christ by bearing another's burden, is to be *in* joy and by his Spirit to be *a* joy.

He emptied himself

In all this Christ shows us the way. He emptied himself, taking the form of a bondservant. Paul says that we should have the same mind and attitude that was in Christ—that outlook on life where we are delivered from looking after our own interests, being wrapped up in our own concerns, but rather deliberately give ourselves to being concerned and interested in others, 'doing nothing from selfishness or empty conceit'. How wonderfully this was demonstrated in his own life! Paul was a man of joy and although frequently in circumstances which, in the natural way, would suffocate joy, yet he rejoiced in the Lord and urged all believers to do the same. When he wrote those memorable words to the church at Philippi, 'Rejoice in the Lord always; again I will say, rejoice!' he was in prison and he did not know if he would be released to continue his ministry or be put to death for Christ's sake. It looked very much as though his life would be poured out as a drink offering upon the sacrifice and service of their faith (Phil 2:17). Faith, also, for these believers meant sacrifice and service and for Paul himself to such a degree that his life, like a drink offering, would be emptied to the last dregs. He, like the Lord Jesus, emptied himself. But he was in no way despondent about this. Once again, his irrepressible joy in the Lord breaks through. 'I rejoice and share my joy with you all' (Phil 2:17). The flesh shrinks from sacrifice but faith and love rejoice to follow Christ in this and in following find more joy, enough and to spare.

Those who serve from emptied hearts have given up grasping. Jesus, though co-equal with the Father and the Holy Spirit, for our sakes and for our salvation emptied himself of his divine glory and attributes. 'He . . . did not regard equality with God a thing to be grasped' (Phil 2:6)— though he had every right to do so. He surrendered freely, yielding his divine dignity for our sakes. True servants have given over grasping, revelling in position, coveting status, hankering for recognition. How easy it is to become possessive, even in the work of the Lord, so that we can cling to *our* work, *our* ministry, *our* church, *our* reputation. How different was the attitude of the Lord Jesus who emptied himself and humbled himself. He came, not to be served, but to serve. He did not come among us as an official or ecclesiastical dignitary. He did not come courting the praises of men. He said, 'I do not receive glory from men' and added, 'How can you believe, when you receive glory from one another, and you do not seek the glory that is from the one and only God?' (Jn 5:41, 44). He did not come as the brash, top executive of a multi-million corporation, presiding over a workforce who are mere numbers on the payroll. No, he himself was the worker, the servant, the slave. So we see him in the gospels, not telling the disciples what to do but showing them by his own example. How powerfully John sets the scene in his gospel:

> Jesus, *knowing that the Father had given all things into His hands,* and that He had come forth from God, and was going back to God, rose from supper, and laid aside His garments; and taking a towel, He girded Himself about. Then He poured water into the basin, and began to wash his disciples' feet, and wipe them with the towel with which He was girded . . . And so, when He had washed their feet, and taken His garments, and reclined at table again, He said to them, 'Do you know what I have done to you? You call Me Teacher and Lord; and you are right, for so I am. If I then, the Lord and the Teacher, washed your feet, you also ought to wash one another's feet. For I gave you an example that you also should do as I did to you. Truly, truly, I say to you, a slave is not greater than his master; neither is one who is sent greater than the one who sent him. If you know these things, you are blessed if you do them' (Jn 13:3–5, 12–17).

He shows them that the secret of blessedness, of happiness, is in serving.

Let us look now at some of the ways in which we can serve the Lord with joy. First, by ministering to the Lord. This is at the heart of all vital service for God—to seek the face of God, to wait in his presence, to get our strength renewed or our way made clear, to delight ourselves in the Lord—this is to be preferred above all other delights. We share his heart and concerns and allow ourselves to be so moved by the Holy Spirit that we are enabled to make intercession for the saints according to the will of God. Perhaps you say that you are no expert at praying. I know—neither am

I, for there are no prayer experts. It is written of us all—'we do not know how to pray as we should'. If you find that consoling, here is something even better—'The Spirit also helps our weakness' (Rom 8:26) and he enables us to make intercession. Paul makes mention of Epaphrus, a bond-slave of Jesus Christ, 'always laboring earnestly for you in his prayers, that you may stand perfect and fully assured in all the will of God' (Col 4:12). What a service! This kind of labour must be at the heart of all that we seek to do for God.

Our ministering to the Lord will pre-eminently be a time when we cultivate our love relationship with the Lord Jesus. We shall hear him say, 'Do you love me?' and if, like Peter, we reply, 'Lord, You know all things; You know that I love You,' we shall hear him say, 'Tend my sheep'—which we may freely interpret in this way. 'If you love me, take care of mine. Look after what belongs to me. Let nothing be too much trouble to do for those who are mine. Do everything you can for them, but do it because you love me.' Is this not what Paul meant when he said that the love of Christ compelled him? And will it not be a crowning joy to hear the Saviour say to us one day, 'As you did it to one of the least of these my brethren, you did it to me' (Mt 25:40, RSV). For serving out of love for Jesus will deliver us from picking and choosing or chafing because we would prefer to do something else other than that which the Lord has assigned us. We shall be only too happy to do anything for the Lord.

John Newton is reputed to have said that if God summoned two angels, ordering one to preach the gospel and the other to sweep the roads, it would be a matter of utter indifference as to which task they did. Their joy would be to do what God had asked them to do. So it will be with us when what we do is done out of love for Christ. Whatever the task may be it will be done thoroughly, conscientiously and in a manner worthy of the Lord.

Many who find their ordinary jobs tedious and boring and their circumstances difficult would approach the office or factory with new zeal and delight if they went with the realization that they worked, not first of all for their employer, but for their divine Lord and Master and rendered their service to him. A mother bringing up her children for God (and what a tremendous ministry *that* is!) will find an added joy as she hears the Lord say, 'Take this child . . . and nurse him for me' (Ex 2:9).

One of the sadder characteristics of this present decade is the increase in the number of unemployed. This is an economic and social problem that is widespread both in this country and overseas. But in the kingdom of God none need be unemployed. Every believer has some talent to trade with, all have some gift with which they can bless the body of Christ. Everyone has a place and part in the eternal purpose of God.

Serving the church

This is seen clearly in the pages of the New Testament. The saints were anointed with the Holy Spirit, fired with love for God and seen devoting themselves to one another in love. They lived and moved among a veritable epidemic of 'one anotherism'. Again and again the words meet us in the New Testament—love one another, care for one another, pray for one another, teach and admonish one another. The references for looking up 'one another' would fill a page, and what a transformation would be evident in our local churches if we lived in such an environment where every member stirred up the gift of God within them, traded with the talent the Lord has entrusted to them for the enrichment of their fellow believers, and showed themselves a people for God's own possession, zealous in good works.

Let us avoid the error of thinking of Christian service in terms only of public teaching and preaching. Platform ministry is but a small part of the variety of ministries and gifts set in the body of Christ. The gifts of God are as variegated as his variegated grace. There is ministry that is apostolic or prophetic; there is the ministry of the evangelist or teacher. But there is also administration, giving, hospitality and that much underrated but marvellously practical gift of helps—an all-embracing word to cover a whole spectrum of love-inspired and love-imparting service.

While visiting a fellowship recently, I was handed a cake made by one of the ladies of the church. I remember that the same thing had happened on a previous occasion. Such kindness blessed me enormously but I was further blessed to hear that she did this for all visiting preachers, who in the same way were regaled with her delicious home-made cakes. But I was even more blessed and gladdened to hear that this same lady had made it her concern to find out the particular need or interest of every other person in the church and, within a year, every member of that fellowship had been on the receiving end of her kindness which was shown in a variety of ways. Everyone was blessed with some token of her love and kindness. What an example! What a blessing! And what a joy! The holy women who ministered to Jesus of their substance shared to the full in his ministry as much as the apostles who were preaching and healing the sick.

Serving the world

After his resurrection and before he ascended into heaven, Jesus said, 'Go ye into all the world, and preach the gospel to every creature' (Mk 16: 15, AV). We are to 'make disciples of all the nations' (Mt 28:19). To move in obedience to his mandate means that we take not only his message but his presence. For his assurance is that as we go, 'I am with you.' Such a commissioning should save us from settling into evangelical ghettoes and shutting ourselves away, cut off from those who need to hear the word of God. We are left in the world for a deliberate purpose and intent—to be light in its darkness and salt amidst its corrupting influences. We are to do good to all men, letting our light shine before them that they may see our good works and glorify our Father in heaven. And especially we are to abound in those works which Jesus referred to when he said, 'The works that I do, shall [you] do also; and greater works than these shall [you] do' (Jn 14:12). In thinking of the nations, let us not overlook the people who live in the same street. God has sent us to them. Let us get amongst them, let us go where people are, let us invade the pubs and clubs, let us take the offensive for God, let us go as the seventy went—proclaiming the kingdom and healing the sick. Let us watch for God-given opportunities to smile, to talk, to help, to pray, doing all in company with the Lord and proving the joy of the Lord to be our strength.

IO

Joy in Sorrow

In all that I have written about joy I hope it has become clear that Christians are not given a trouble-free life. Don't we all know it! Christ does not promise his followers exemption from trouble or cushion them from the pressures of living in an ungodly world. Rather, he has assured us: 'In the world, you have tribulation'—that is the bad news. But here is the good news—'Take courage; I have overcome the world' (Jn 16:33).

Indeed, for Christians it means that in addition to what men and women face ordinarily by way of suffering there are sufferings and challenges that come simply because we are Christians. This has been the lot of the people of God in all generations. The truth of our Lord's words (above) have been verified again and again. He has overcome the world. Everything in this world by way of sin and suffering has been overcome. Whatever, therefore, may come our way, as believers we never need face them alone. We can count on the presence and help of our great Overcomer. Let the world do its worst—Christ has overcome the world and those who believe in him overcome too (1 Jn 5:4). This is the explanation of Paul's paradoxical statement 'as sorrowful yet always rejoicing' (2 Cor 6:10). On the surface, sorrow and rejoicing are incompatible. You either have one or the other. But Paul declares that he knows both emotions at the same time and many are the evidences for this.

At Philippi, Paul and Silas preached the gospel and we read that a slave-girl who earned her owners a good deal of money by telling fortunes was delivered from an evil spirit. Paul had said, 'I command you in the name of Jesus Christ to come out of her!' and instantly she was set free from that demonic power which gave her the ability to tell fortunes. The owners were incensed and dragged Paul and his companion before the magistrates on false charges. The mob rose up against them, the magistrates ordered them to be beaten and they were thrown into prison, their feet held fast in the stocks. That record is a typical example of the tribulation that the early believers knew. They were frequently deprived of their liberty for Christ's sake, and all down the centuries it has been true. Many of God's saints—people like John Bunyan—have been imprisoned for their faith. And it is true today. In several parts of the world there are people in prison for no other reason than that they believe in the Lord Jesus and desire to be faithful to him. But when God's people go to prison, they take their joy with them. They rejoice to be counted worthy to suffer for Christ's name and fellowship with him in their suffering (cf. Phil 3:10). So Paul and Silas, we read, were praying and singing hymns of praise to God. Their liberty was gone but their joy no man could take from them.

Likewise, the believers could rejoice in the loss of their property. When we open the letter to the Hebrews, we find that the writer makes reference to this—that the believers of that time accepted joyfully the seizure of their property (Heb 10:34). This was part of the great conflict of sufferings which they had to endure.

Let us think about that for a moment. In the normal way it is not an easy thing to bear injustice and indignity, but these were meted out to the early Christians while others, who opposed them, helped themselves to what rightly did not belong to them. Yet the Christians were able to take this all in their stride and to do so joyfully.

The same was true of the believers to whom Peter wrote. He said they were 'distressed by various trials' yet were enabled to rejoice greatly and to such a degree that he calls it 'joy inexpressible and full of glory' (1 Pet 1:6,8). It was a joy that conveyed the very bliss of heaven and more than compensated for any loss or deprivation they suffered.

Sometimes it was life itself that these believers were called to yield. The noble army of martyrs not only died in faith, they died in joy. Time and again as you read the records of these men and women going to be crucified or thrown to the lions, burned at the stake or beheaded, they—like Stephen before them—have known such clear visions of the glory of God and Jesus standing at the right hand of God, that the word of God became their experience. 'If you are reviled for the name of Christ, you are blessed, because the Spirit of glory and of God rests upon you' (1 Pet 4:14). Or as Paul puts it, 'We also exult in our tribulations' (Rom 5:3).

We read of the martyr, Roland Taylor, on his way to being burned at the stake.

All the way Taylor was joyful and happy as one that accounted himself going to a most pleasant banquet or bridal feast. He spoke many notable things to the sheriff and the yeomen of the guard that conducted him, and often moved them to weep through his earnest calling upon them to repent and to amend their evil and wicked living. Often also he caused them to wonder and rejoice to see him constant and steadfast, devoid of all fear, joyful in heart and glad to die.[12]

Jesus spoke one of his most significant utterances on joy in the sermon on the mount. 'Blessed are those who have been persecuted for the sake of righteousness, for theirs is the kingdom of heaven. Blessed are you when men cast insults at you, and say all kinds of evil against you falsely, on account of Me. Rejoice, and be glad, for your reward in heaven is great, for so they persecuted the prophets who were before you' (Mt 5:10–12). Luke enlarges and amplifies this statement in his gospel: 'Blessed are you when men hate you and ostracize you, and cast insults at you, and spurn your name as evil, for the sake of the Son of Man. Be glad in that day, and leap for joy, for behold, your reward is great in heaven; for in the same way their fathers used to treat the prophets' (Lk 6:22–23).

Here, it seems to me, the supernatural element is introduced again, for ordinarily it would be difficult and, indeed, well-nigh impossible to rejoice when ostracized, insulted and persecuted. But the Spirit of glory and of God comes upon us. The worst afflictions are transfigured. They not only rejoice, but do so with joy unspeakable and full of glory. To quote again what is said of Roland Taylor, he 'accounted himself going to a most pleasant banquet or bridal feast'. He could rightly have used the well-known words of the psalm—'Thou dost prepare a table before me in the presence of my enemies; Thou hast anointed my head with oil; my cup overflows' (Ps 23:5). At the time of greatest need—when reviled, persecuted, facing death—the joy of the Lord became their strength. And we have such an abundant supply promised us, such a surplus of heavenly bliss, that should we be called upon to suffer we can be exceeding glad and leap for joy.

Cheer up!

Sometimes we have days when seemingly everything goes wrong and nothing goes right. 'It's just one of those days,' we say. On such a day it is no help for some exuberant friend to come along with a breezy greeting and a slap on the back, saying, 'Cheer up! It may never happen.' The cynical might be tempted to reply, 'On the other hand, it may and in the light of what has happened today—it probably will!'

Jesus, when on earth, frequently used the words 'Cheer up'—'Be of good cheer'. But he never used them without giving solid reasons for taking heart and renewed courage. And the reason he gave was: 'Be of good cheer; *it is I; be not afraid*' (Mt 14:27, AV). Again and again he uttered these words against the backcloth of human need, nervousness and distress. When the disciples were terrified by the storm, when the palsied man was helpless and desperate for healing, when Bartimaeus was asking for his eyes to be opened—to each of these Jesus said, 'Be of good cheer.' It lifted their spirits for it heralded the intervention of his power, giving them the courage to cope. For the greeting of cheer was undergirded with the words '. . . it is I; be not afraid'.

When we know that the one who has overcome is with us, that puts our whole situation, whatever it may be, in a completely new perspective. If the Son of God is on the scene his presence is sufficient to banish all fear. For with him as our strength and our song we can be of good cheer whatever our circumstances.

Circumstances vary of course—sometimes they are very humdrum as life goes on day by day in the same old routine, week after week, month after weary month. That can be very demoralizing and boring. Or our circumstances can be a source of frustration as we never seem to be able to achieve our ambitions or reach the goals we are striving for. We put ourselves well and truly among the failures of life. For others, life can be hard indeed as they suffer the 'slings and arrows of outrageous fortune'—disappointment, treachery, bereavement can devastate the heart. But whatever our circumstances, if the living Christ is present speaking this courage-imparting word then we shall triumph.

This was the conviction of the apostle Paul: 'Who shall separate us from the love of Christ? Shall tribulation, or distress, or persecution, or famine, or nakedness, or peril, or sword?' (Rom 8:35). He seems, with these questions, to throw down the gauntlet, challenging all the forces of evil to do their worst. His confidence in Christ is complete. In all these things we overwhelmingly conquer through him who loves us.

Whatever our circumstances, therefore, we need not allow them to master us but, in Christ, we must master them. If our situation is grim it is always good to face the facts. Pretending they are not there will not send them away! The Christian believer is a realist and he can face the facts however dark and black they may be, for he remembers that God is always greater than the facts. God has the power, the illimitable resources, the wisdom that can either change the circumstances or use them to foster our growth in grace, or overrule them so that amazingly our liabilities become assets, our enemies become allies and obstacles become a highway for his eternal purpose. If anything should cheer us, it is the certain knowledge that 'all things . . . work together for good to those who love God, to those who are called according to His purpose' (Rom 8:28).

How clearly this is seen in a man like Joseph. If anyone knew about trying circumstances it was Joseph. He knew ridicule, hatred, treachery, misrepresentation, imprisonment. Yet throughout his life, though he seemed to be thrown into seas of sorrows and the waves and billows threatened to overwhelm him again and again, he never drowned. There was an amazing buoyancy about his life. It seems to me he had a soul made of spiritual cork, wave after wave washed over him but every time he bobbed up again. His brothers put him down—he rose again. He went down in the household of Potiphar when Potiphar's wife accused him unjustly—he came up again. In the prison he went down but eventually rose again until, finally, he was virtual ruler of Egypt. What was his secret? It is summed up in a brief but significant phrase: 'The Lord was with Joseph' (Gen 39:21). Through the Lord he was more than conqueror.

Jesus has promised his church: 'I am with you *always*,' or as the Revised Version margin puts it, 'all the days'. Whatever sort of day it may be—rainy or sunny, sad or glad—this truth transforms them all. 'I am with you. Be of good cheer.'

11

Joy in Trouble

So far we have looked at sorrow largely in the context of persecutions suffered for Christ's sake and the gospel's. But there is another kind of suffering which is more common to those of us who live in the West. For today we do not face harassment from the state or being pelted with stones or garbage when we preach the gospel in the streets. In the liberty won for us by our fore-fathers, who *did* suffer in this way, we have complete freedom to believe and preach the gospel of Christ. Our sorrows come from life's events. We share with all mankind the common lot of living in a fallen world. When we come to consider the appalling calamities that can befall men and women, we need always to keep in mind that this world is a fallen world. It is not as it was created. It is not as God meant it to be or yet how it will be. That being so, things can go disastrously wrong. It is a world where there are wars and rumours of wars, diseases and plagues, a world of violence, bloodshed and lust.

In other words, a fallen world is a sinful world. Sin has caused the very natural order to be distorted so in the world we are exposed to natural perils, such as earthquakes, famines and floods. In addition, we are surrounded with increasing evidence of 'man's inhumanity to man' that results in robbery, rape and murder. And so, in this topsy-turvy world there are such things as accidents, illnesses, losses and appalling tragedies. Christians do not escape entirely from these common sorrows. Job records that 'man is born for trouble, as sparks fly upward' (Job 5:7). The troubles of man come to all men and women, irrespective of whether they are Christians or not. In speaking of the providence of God, Jesus said that our Father causes his sun to rise on the evil and the good, that he sends rain on the righteous and the unrighteous. Just as the blessings of God in nature are given to men, irrespective of their spiritual state or condition, so the troubles of the world come to us as men living in this present, evil world.

Devastating troubles

And what devastating troubles can come our way! The middle-aged man with a growing family suddenly confronted with the news that he has incurable cancer; the young couple faced with the sudden horror of their baby's cot death; the teenager involved in a motorcycle accident, damaging his spine paralysing him for life. Or it can be trouble of a different sort, all too common in our time but nevertheless bringing acute pain and grief—i.e. the wife or husband who finds themself abandoned because their partner has gone to live with someone else. These calamities bring heavy sorrow in and of themselves but, in addition, our minds can be tortured because there seems to be a terrible injustice about life's cruel blows. These things seem haphazard, striking people at random and without reason. Frequently in such circumstances the cry is heard: 'What have I done to deserve this?' And in our answers we add the burden of guilt to our already saddened hearts, or we begin to doubt the love and wisdom of God. God, we affirm, is just. Where is the justice in all this?

Job met headlong one disaster after another, losing his family, his home, his possessions and his health. And, added to all his sufferings, was the pain of sheer perplexity. Why? There did not seem to be any reason or purpose. We know now that there was, but at the time he was ignorant of this. It left him baffled and bewildered, and in times of tragedy we find ourselves in the same situation.

It seems so futile

Another factor which intensifies our suffering is the seeming futility of it all. You can accept the situation more easily if you can detect some meaning of purpose, but many things that come our way seem so pointless: the child born with spina bifida or Down's syndrome, or the aged relative stricken with senile dementia. It takes a major and massive adjustment of the heart and mind to come to terms with such a situation. Christians who suffered for Christ's sake and the gospel's had a glorious cause, indeed, the greatest cause, to give them uplift and inspiration in what they were enduring. They were inspired by the fact of being right in the purpose of God and in the absolute certainty of the ultimate triumph of his kingdom. In many of life's troubles we cannot discern any purpose or reason and that important dimension is missing. Can we then rejoice in times of such trouble?

The Bible has no doubt that a Christian can and should rejoice at all times, that in all sorts of conditions and circumstances he should be rejoicing evermore. The circumstances may be grievous and the crisis of mammoth proportions, and in no way are we insulated from the pain and the sorrow that these conditions bring. Indeed, you feel them and feel them keenly as Jesus did when he wept at the grave of Lazarus. But the Christian can rejoice in the Lord who, whatever has happened or will happen, never leaves us or forsakes us. He is a very present help in trouble.

When dark days are upon us it is the greatest possible benefit in seeing our way through to joy to have the light of God's word shining upon our circumstances. Frequently, we add to our sufferings by ignorance of the guiding principles of God's written word. In time of trouble it is especially important that we rid our minds of some common misconceptions. Let us deal with one or two of them.

Suffering and sin

First, suffering is never a punishment for sin. Many people think that all calamities and crises are some kind of retribution for their wrong-doing—that the Almighty's government is a kind of rough justice. But life in general does not bear this out and Jesus taught plainly that this was not so. When dealing with the man born blind and giving him his sight, the Lord was asked by his disciples whether the man had sinned or his parents. Jesus gave a categorical answer to that. He said, 'Neither.' It was not a condition that had come about as a direct consequence of sin. But there are those still who immediately connect calamity or illness and distress with sin and its punishment. This was the short-sighted view of Job's comforters, who seemed to take an unholy delight in telling him that all his misfortunes were his own fault. They could not have been more wrong, for God had said of his servant, 'There is no one like him on the earth, a blameless and upright man, fearing God and turning away from evil' (Job 1:8).

On the other hand we read of our Lord's dealings with the man he met at Bethesda, a place where the physically afflicted were congregating. This man had been ill for thirty-eight years and, with a command, the Lord Jesus raised him to health again, enabling the man to stand, take up his mattress and walk away carrying the mattress that had carried him. Later, Jesus met him in the temple and said to him, 'Behold, you have become well; do not sin anymore, so that nothing worse may befall you' (Jn 5:14). It seems clear from what the Lord says here that this man's sickness was related to some specific sin. This is reinforced by the warning that further sin could bring further and greater trouble. Then again, the apostle Paul makes it clear that the disorders in the church at Corinth had brought physical weakness and sickness upon some of its members (1 Cor 11:30).

In the light of this, it would seem that sometimes there is a direct link between sin and suffering, but this is not always the case. All suffering is the result of sin in the ultimate sense (see Gen 3) but personal suffering is not necessarily the result of personal sin. The wise will tread very cautiously here, not wanting to bring added pain to those already suffering by making false and foolish connections, remembering that some of the most godly people that have ever lived have had to endure many afflictions and have done so with a magnificent testimony to the grace of God and a joy in the Lord that has blessed and refreshed all who came into contact with them.

Cause and effect

In saying this, we do not overlook the fact that many of the troubles of mankind are self-inflicted. Men do, at times, bring trouble on themselves. The drug addict poisons his own body and blows his own mind; the sexually promiscuous person risks contracting venereal disease; the workaholic, burning with zeal to succeed, is vulnerable to coronary trouble; and those who harbour resentment and nurse their grudges find that these festering thoughts react upon their bodies in various ways. We know that every Christmas the festivities are overshadowed by the injury or death of road casualties due to drunken drivers. In such human folly we see the outworking of the natural law of cause and effect. It is not God meting out vindictive punishment or calling us to pay for our sins. Nothing that we can bear by way of suffering, nothing that we can endure in this life or the next, can make atonement for sin. Atonement for sin is not by human suffering but by the self-offering and sinless sacrifice of the Lord Jesus on the cross. The Lord has laid on *him* the iniquity of us all. If we imagine that in some way we can make atonement ourselves or add to Christ's sacrifice by our pains and tribulations, we rob him and his once-for-all offering for sin of its singular and unique glory.

Joy in the cross

We read that Jesus endured the cross 'for the joy set before Him' (Heb 12:2) and that cross, in all its grim horror, became the scene of his greatest triumph and the basis of all our joys. In his darkest hour he found the way through to joy. There is always joy in doing God's will and though it meant for Jesus the most horrific experience of being 'made sin', yet he determined to press on whatever the personal cost. His joy, too, was before him in the sense that sin and all its fearful consequences would be overthrown, death would be defeated, the works of the devil destroyed and the way opened for man to receive forgiveness of sin and to be transferred from the kingdom of darkness to live in God's marvellous light.

There was another ingredient of our Lord's joy, for the cross was not the end. God raised him from the dead and exalted him to his own right hand and with joy he contemplated the sending forth of the Spirit of power and the building of his church and the establishing of God's kingdom in the earth. He could see the ultimate and total overthrow of sin and the devil; his coming again in glory when every earthly wrong would be put right; the complete destruction of sin, disease and pain; the creation of a new heaven and a new earth where righteousness will dwell. And what brought such joy to Jesus should bring joy to us. Whatever sorrows we may be enduring now, things will not always be as they are. The cross is the guarantee that one day all tears will be wiped away. There is a joy set before us that will more than compensate for the troubles we have now. As Paul puts it:

> For I consider that the sufferings of this present time are not worthy to be compared with the glory that is to be revealed to us. For the anxious longing of the creation waits eagerly for the revealing of the sons of God. For the creation was subjected to futility, not of its own will, but because of him who subjected it, in hope that the creation itself also will be set free from its slavery to corruption into the freedom of the glory of the children of God (Rom 8:18–21).

So better and glorious times, then, are coming. Let us share the Lord's joy in the sure prospect that the whole creation will be utterly divested of all the relics of sin and its curse.

In the meantime, it pleases the Lord, even in the midst of this creation bound in its slavery to corruption, to display his power in miracles and signs and wonders. Even now, to anticipate that day when all wrongs will be righted and diseases banished, God will heal the sick, cure the incurable and deliver his saints. The kingdom that is coming is already here. It sounds paradoxical but it is a fact. It does not come, nor consist, in words, but in power. John Wimber has put this so cogently in his book *Power Evangelism:*

> Miracles are a foreshadowing and promise of coming universal redemption and the fullness of the kingdom. Casting out demons signals God's invasion of the realm of Satan and Satan's final destruction (Matthew 12:29, Mark 3:27; Luke 11:21ff; John 12:31; Revelation 20:1ff). Healing the sick bears witness to the end of all suffering (Revelation 21:4). Miraculous provisions of food tell us about the end of all human need (Revelation 7:16ff). Stilling storms points forward to the complete victory over the powers of nature that threaten the earth. Raising the dead announces that death will be forever done away with (1 Corinthians 15:26).[13]

Let us then have faith for God to intervene in our circumstances. How true and timeless is the word of the Lord: 'Is anyone among you suffering? Let him pray. Is anyone cheerful? Let him sing praises. Is any among you sick? Let him call for the elders of the church, and let them pray over him, anointing him with oil in the name of the Lord; and the prayer offered in faith will restore the one who is sick, and the Lord will raise him up' (Jas 5:13–15). Many are the testimonies that the Lord is doing such wonders today.

But you may say, 'I *have* prayed and healing hasn't come.' Yes, I myself have known many situations like that. It would be foolish to deny the fact that many have been anointed and prayed for and they have not recovered. I do not pretend to understand or have the answers to this problem. There is a mystery about suffering that baffles the human mind. But God has impressed upon me that I should never let past disappointments dent my faith for present needs. So I hold fast to the word of God—'the prayer of faith will save [mg.] the one who is sick'—and seek to bring to each case fresh faith in the living God and his faithful word. I have prayed for some to be healed and seemingly nothing has happened. I have prayed for others and they have been healed immediately and dramatically, while yet others have been healed gradually. I do not know why some are healed and others are not, but I know I am called to believe and obey the word of God. And if our healing seems to be denied or delayed, let us find joy in the abundant grace the Lord Jesus supplies. His grace is always commensurate with our need. It is always sufficient, enabling us to reign over our circumstances through grace.

If we have joy in what our Lord suffered for us on the cross we can rejoice too in what he is doing for us now. Reigning supreme at the right hand of God, he is sovereignly overruling our lives. Nothing comes our way without his permission, and whatever he permits is part of his purpose.

He will take all things and turn them to our good and for his own glory. And when the going is tough and rough, he is aware of our situation, he feels for us in our weakness and, as our sympathizing high priest, he ever lives to make intercession for us (Heb 7:25).

I remember vividly when this text became a practical reality in my life. Weakened by a long illness that showed no sign of abating but was getting worse, I reached the point where being so utterly bereft of physical strength I could no longer read the Bible or even pray. This caused me some concern and then suddenly these words came flooding into my heart, 'He ever lives to make intercession for you.' And I knew, in a way I had not known before, that Jesus was praying for me. Suddenly the hospital room was flooded with the presence of God. I felt as if I was lifted and cradled in the very arms of God. It was one of the most amazing experiences of my life. I understood better the doxology of Paul: 'Blessed be the God and Father of our Lord Jesus Christ, the Father of mercies and God of all comfort; who comforts us in all our affliction so that we may be able to comfort those who are in any affliction, with the comfort with which we ourselves are comforted by God' (2 Cor 1:3–4). And I relate this experience now for that very purpose, that some who read these words may be truly comforted by God. We have a great high priest, touched with the feeling of our infirmities and, as the old hymn-writer puts it: 'His heart is made of tenderness, it overflows with love.' In that, we find our joy.

12

Watch Out for the Killjoys!

A life of joy will not go unnoticed by the devil or be allowed to exist unopposed by him, so be prepared! He comes to kill and destroy. He will seek to destroy our confidence in God, our communication *with* God in prayer and thus to kill our joy in some way, or to mar or limit it.

One of the evil one's great subtleties is that, in approaching us, he makes it seem as if he has our interests at heart. He tells us that he only desires what is best—he wants our happiness. But nothing could be further from the truth. He is a liar and he could not care less about our happiness, but so subtle are his approaches that we fall for this ploy again and again. Actually, he designs to plague us with miseries so he will use any means to achieve this. He will goad us and lure us into sin, exploiting our natural weaknesses, appealing to our old natures, piling on the pressure, suggesting again and again to us that we are missing out by not indulging in the pleasures of sin.

'Everybody else is doing it,' he tells us. 'You deserve to live life to the full. Why should you be restricted in what you do? You have a right to be happy and do what you want.' In this way, he overcomes whatever measure of resistance we seek to put up. Then, the moment we yield, he turns and rounds upon us with a veritable fusillade of condemnation. 'What, you? A Christian? Acting like that! You don't think that God will continue to love you after doing *that*! Surely God will now cast you away and tire of you.'

How clever the enemy is! Don't be ignorant of his devices or listen to his specious arguments. Sin can never be to our good and it is always detrimental to our joy, for it mars our fellowship with Father, it dishonours the name of the Lord Jesus and it grieves the Holy Spirit of God. Thank God that there is a marvellous provision for us. 'If anyone sins we have an Advocate with the Father. If we confess our sins, He is faithful and righteous to forgive us our sins and to cleanse us from all unrighteousness' (1 Jn 1:9). In reading those words, don't think for one moment that forgiveness is something slick and easy. You could not be more wrong. No Christian can sin without loss and the first thing he loses is his joy. He knows again the weight of the spirit of heaviness with a vengeance.

Look at David confessing his sin (Ps 51). He was, as the saying goes, as miserable as sin. He compares his misery to the pain of a broken bone and he is prepared for God to do anything so long as God will restore to him the joy of his salvation. So he prays, 'Wash me, cleanse me, purge me, create in me a new heart, make me to hear joy and gladness.' Yes, sin is a killjoy. Avoid it like the plague. Whatever the devil says about it, it will rob you of your Father's smile and therefore of your joy. Certainly the Lord can restore the joy of his salvation to us, but better still he can maintain us in joy by keeping us from evil and enabling us to overcome the evil one. The words are true, '[He is] able to keep you from stumbling and to make you stand in the presence of His glory blameless with great joy' (Jude 24).

Breakdown in love

One particular sin the devil employs to rob us of our joy is to bring division, misunderstanding and distrust between believers. If he can set them quarrelling, biting and devouring one another, so much the better. What a fruitful field the church has been for the enemy to sow seeds of hatred, setting brother against brother, Christian against Christian. What a sad and sorry record of bickering, bitterness, estrangement has blighted the testimony of the people of God. We have shut our eyes to the truths of God's word that whatever we may boast of concerning our gifts, our calling or expertise, if we do not have love we have nothing. We have shut our ears to the words of Jesus: 'Just as the Father has loved Me, I have also loved you; abide in My love. If you keep My commandments you will abide in My love; just as I have kept My Father's commandments, and abide in His love. These things I have spoken to you, that My joy may be in you, and that your joy may be made full. This is My commandment, that you love one another, just as I have loved you' (Jn 15:9–12).

What Christ is saying here is that we prove our love for him by keeping his commands. In this way we know the bliss of living in his love. And his command is that we love one another in the same sacrificial way that he has loved us. This will result in his joy being in us—the joy he has of living in his Father's love and delighting to do his commands—and our joy shall be full.

So if we are to know and maintain fullness of joy we must be aware of causing any breach of love, for this will bring a swift decline in the measure of our joy.

Dealing with hurt

At some time or another we will be wronged, or believe we have been wronged, and it is an added thorn if we are wronged by those we thought were our friends. Let us be especially careful how we react to such treatment for it is true that it is *not* what happens to us that is so important but how we react to what happens. We need the grace of Christ to calm our spirits, to curb the hasty word and to control our actions. 'He who is slow to anger is better than the mighty, and he who rules his spirit, than he who captures a city' (Prov 16:32).

Dealing with breakdown

Where breakdown in relationship is threatened, the correct procedure is wisely set out for us by the Lord Jesus himself. 'If your brother sins against you, go and show him his fault, just between the two of you [literally, between you and him alone]' (Mt 18:15, NIV). So we seek out the brother privately. And this is the first major mistake frequently made. For often the last person we go to is the individual concerned, and in doing so we compound the problem. Before we consult with anyone else we should see the person involved and endeavour to get the matter settled between him and ourselves. In face-to-face confrontation, misunderstandings can be ironed out, apologies can be made and love can be avowed afresh. Should it be that you cannot resolve matters together then others can be brought in. Should the problem seem intractable after that, it is to be brought to the church for them to bring judgement.

The essential point in all this is that breakdown in fellowship is a serious matter and must not be allowed to dribble on like a dripping tap needing a new washer. No, the issue must be resolved and where there is genuine love for the Lord and his people, Christians in dispute will fall over backwards to be reconciled. They will be only too ready to admit their wrong, apologize and make amends. Likewise the offended one will be only too pleased to forgive and forget, to embrace his reconciled brother and to encourage him in God. Such demonstrated love will fill them with this double joy that Jesus speaks of—'These things I have spoken to you, that *My joy* may be in you, and that *your joy* may be made full' (Jn 15:11).

The forgiving heart

For this to happen we must maintain a forgiving spirit. 'Be kind to one another, tender-hearted, forgiving each other, just as God in Christ also has forgiven you' (Eph 4:32). Having been forgiven should make it ever so easy for us to forgive others. The fact that God has cancelled my enormous debt of millions of pounds should make it easy for me to cancel the debt of a few miserly pence that my brother owes me. And yet, many who claim to be forgiven have failed in this matter of extending forgiveness to others. I believe such people need to be delivered from a strong delusion. Jesus said, 'If you do not forgive men, then your Father will not forgive your transgressions' (Mt 6:15). Where we keep old scores, cherish our grudges, allow hurts to fester, there is a real danger of a root of bitterness taking hold of our hearts. Such people are sad and they minister sadness. The bitterness of their spirit comes through their conversation, their actions and even their ministry.

One day at school, we were having a geography lesson and the master brought to the classroom a wooden cup which he had acquired during his travels overseas. He proceeded to fill this cup with water and then invited us to drink. I remember tasting and immediately being aware of a sense of revulsion as the acrid liquid smarted on my palate. It was vile! The cup, he explained, was a quassia cup made from the wood of a certain tree and whatever fluid you put into it partook of the bitterness of the wood. There are lives that can be likened to that quassia cup. They have become so embittered that they permeate the atmosphere around and impregnate all that they touch with the bitterness of their own hearts. They have allowed life's hurts to sour them so that all life's events are tinctured with bitterness. To be embittered in this way is to stifle all joy in ourselves and, indeed, in others. Our calling and our responsibility is to forgive, and to forgive as God has forgiven us—not reluctantly, but gladly; not partially, but fully. The sentiment so often expressed —'I can forgive, but can't forget'—falls far, far, short of the forgiveness that God extends to us. He declares, 'I will forgive their iniquity, and their sin I will remember no more' (Jer 31:34).

Living in his love, keeping his commands, we are called to love as he loved us. Most of us are familiar with the truth that God loves a cheerful giver, which is frequently rendered as God loves a 'hilarious' giver. When Paul writes to the Roman Christians, he urges them to show mercy with cheerfulness (Rom 12:14), using the same root of the word as is translated 'cheerful' or 'hilarious'. So we may say that God not only loves the hilarious giver but also the hilarious *for*giver. Such hilarity must be seen among us in abundant measure.

Timewasting

Another more subtle way that the devil deprives us of joy is to get us to dissipate our time. Time is given us by God and it is a gift that we must use wisely. Paul explains wisdom as 'making the most of your time, because the days are evil' (Eph 5:16). We can translate this 'buying up the opportunities'. The unfolding hours are opportunities given to us to glorify God, but to squander our moments and days in trivialities is a fruitful cause of joylessness. Even on the human level, to have a sense of purpose is very fulfilling and it is tremendous to be able to plan work on a given project, battle against all the difficulties and setbacks and finally see the whole thing brought to completion. Every Christian should live a planned life. The joyous thing is that God has planned it: 'For we are His workmanship, created in Christ Jesus for good works, which God prepared beforehand, that we should walk in them' (Eph 2:10).

Winston Churchill in the nadir of the country's fortunes during the war was summoned by the King to become Prime Minister and war leader. He records his strange emotions—though things were at their lowest ebb, he had a sense of elation in his heart. He writes: 'I felt as if I were walking with destiny, and that all of my past life had been but a preparation for this hour.'[14] Every believer should walk with that sense of high destiny. God directs our paths, he orders our steps, he causes us to walk in his foreordained way and plan. When we give ourselves with enthusiasm to do his will and throw ourselves wholeheartedly and unceasingly to complete all that he has prepared for us, it affords us a joyous sense of achievement and satisfaction. Each of us should have the ambition to live so that at the end of life's day we can say, as the Lord Jesus could say, '[I have] accomplished the work which Thou hast given Me to do' (Jn

17:4). The apostle Paul likewise could say, 'I have fought the good fight, I have finished the course, I have kept the faith' (2 Tim 4:7).

To turn our hours into opportunities will mean that we shall have to discipline our lives so as to make the most of our time, otherwise our hours will be eroded by unwise and unfruitful activities or merely spent in daydreaming. All too often we hear the lame excuse, 'I don't have time' when the simple fact is that God has given us all the time we need for doing what *he* wants us to do. For many of us our lives are cluttered with activities that God does not want us to be involved in and did not plan that we should do, so that we do not have time to do what he really wants us to do.

This calls for an honest appraisal on our part of what we get involved in. We need to be ruthless in seeking out that which whittles away at our precious allotment of time. Jesus laboured in the light of what he could see his Father doing. His diary was not filled with appointments that never had the sanction of God. His motive to minister was not human need or human pressure but the will of God. We shall never succeed in redeeming the time until we are resolute about this.

Mismanagement of time is a fruitful cause of depression, while there is nothing so exhilarating as the discharge of each duty as it presents itself. It can be quite relaxing to view a good TV programme and it is good to do that in conscious fellowship with the Lord, so that if he does not like the programme you switch off! On the other hand, if I devote more and more of my time to the television set, it will rob me of opportunities that could be devoted to prayer. Likewise, it is fine to have a recreation, hobby or sport, but if it gradually takes over my life, taking precedence over God's plan, then it makes me vulnerable. For no believer can keep in joy if he fails to seek first the kingdom of God.

We shall need to add to discipline our diligence. To see a job through from start to finish requires diligence. This implies endeavour and earnestness imbued with a sense of urgency. We are to be diligent about redeeming the time because the days are evil. Therefore, we must be on the alert, stretching all our redeemed powers to get the maximum for God out of each succeeding day. In this way our days will be days of true profit and days of wonderful joy.

13

The Joy of Laughter

This to me is one of the choicest blessings of God. Whether laughter is evoked from pure fun, sparkling wit, a play upon words in repartee, or the sheer sense of the ridiculous, I find that it renews us in spirit and provokes us to thanksgiving to God. Man is unique among the animal creation in that God has created him with the ability to laugh. A. T. Pierson has written: 'If God had not meant us to laugh he would not have put 250 muscles in the human face which are all brought into exercise only in a hearty laugh.'[15] Laughter is the most natural and spontaneous expression of joy.

Not all laughter, of course, is brought about by joy, for both life and the Bible teach us that 'even in laughter the heart may be in pain' (Prov 14:13). There is such a thing as the laughter of fools, which the Bible compares with the crackling of thorns under a pot (Eccles 7:6)—it is all sparks and splutter, making plenty of noise but giving little or no heat. No, the laughter we are speaking of is that which is more than noise. It warms the heart, enlivens the chilly atmosphere with the warmth of cheerfulness and joy and makes the pot of life bubble with renewed fervour and elation.

Causes of laughter

Not only do we have the capacity to laugh but we are living in a world in which we meet with many things that make us laugh. There are, of course, many things which sadden us, that make us weep, but nevertheless there are many things around us that are humorous and we find ourselves dealing with people or events that present themselves in such a way as to reveal the funny side of life. These can and do occur in the most unexpected ways and when they happen it is our instinctive reaction to laugh. There is a time to laugh (Eccles 3:4) and we should thank God for such times. It is true we do not all share the same type of humour. What makes one laugh will not have the same effect upon another. We vary in this as in other matters, but here are some examples taken from actual life that made me laugh.

A friend of mine travelled with a companion to New York. Both of them were preachers reared in a culture of strict teetotalism and they called to see a lady in Manhattan. She was a Presbyterian and, after greeting them, she enquired whether they would like something to drink. This, they assured her, would be most welcome. A little later, after preparing their refreshment, their hostess returned not with coffee cups but—to their aston-ishment—whiskies and soda. Seeing their puzzled expressions and sensing that something was wrong, she handed them the glasses and quietly said, 'Perhaps one of you will give thanks.' I don't know if either of the gentlemen broke into laugh-ter at this point, but I know that I would have!

Spurgeon was a man who loved to laugh, and often this led him to look at situations with a very practical eye. One day a minister came to him for counsel and his problem was a singular one. His tale of woe was this, that whenever he stood up to preach a certain man in the congregation put a finger in one ear and then a finger in the other and sat with both ears blocked for as long as the sermon lasted. He enquired of Spurgeon what he should do about this. Spurgeon, with a straight face, said, 'I should pray.' Then, after a pause he added, 'I should pray that a fly would alight on his nose.'

God, then, has endowed man with the ability to appreciate humour and wit and also to create laughter by this means. Some have a particular and pronounced gift in this and bring added spice to life by creating laughter by their humour. Whilst acknowledging that everything 'may be in-dulged to excess and instead of being a blessing becomes a danger', that is a principle that applies to all other gifts. We should encourage the proper and right use of all natural gifts to the glory of God. Charles Stanford has written for a past generation words that the people of God need to hear today:

Restoring the right use of all natural gifts is included in the idea of salvation. It appears to be a creed not without practical confession that when a man is saved one of the first signs that he is so will be his renunciation of wit and humour. Why? On becoming a Christian why does not the artist give up using one of the painting colours, red, for instance? Or the musician leave out one particular note, say, 'C'. If you must reduce to nothingness one of your own powers of mind or body, why not from that moment blot out one eye or plug one ear, or tie up one leg? Why sacrifice this precious one of wit and humour? Why tell the Creator that he has created within you a sinful energy which you must fight against directly you become a follower of his Son? Believe me, Christ will not destroy that or anything else that helps to make a complete symmetrical man. He came not to destroy but to save. His grace is working in us who are Christians to bring us into complete correspondence with our environment. His religion consists in the right use of man's whole self—not a fibre, not a faculty, not a spark must be left out. The gospel leaves room and kindles fire for the free strong play of all primitive impulses of human nature. It puts its veto on none of them, it only rules and blesses them all.[16]

I feel it is time to appreciate and to thank God for those of ready wit and humour. As one aspect of his liberal giving our God is the one who richly supplies us with all things to enjoy. For too long we have been held prisoner to the views of those who

> Think all virtue lies in gravity
> And smiles are symptoms of depravity.

To be sure, wit and humour can like everything

else be carried to excess and the words of Spurgeon are helpful here: 'Those of us endowed with the dangerous gift of humour need to stop sometimes and take the word out of our mouths and look at it to see whether it is edifying.' Yes, every gift has its dangers but the old principle holds good here—the answer to abuse is not disuse but proper use. If humour and wit are the gifts of God, don't let us put a damper upon them but use them to his glory. To quote Charles Stanford again:

> Do not crush instincts which God has implanted nor ban delights he has provided. Do not torment your own souls or the souls of others gratuitously. In no single thing impose on your own or other's shoulders a Pharisaic yoke. Make no artificial Slough of Despond. Do not, if you can help it, allow any Christian humorist to stand bound and gagged, writhing before his Lord under the impression that this is the way to please Him.[17]

In reviewing the book from which this quotation is taken, Spurgeon comments that 'the whole church will be indebted to Dr Stanford for having protested against the superstition which regards wit and humour as deadly sins. He has not only set forth the propriety of simple, natural mirth but has well nigh shown the duty of it.'

God making us laugh

The Bible records that there are times when God himself makes us laugh. We read that God revealed to Abraham that his barren wife, Sarah, would give birth to a son at the age of ninety, and he himself was one hundred years old. Abraham heard the news with astonishment and 'fell on his face and laughed' (Gen 17:17). He was not in any way censured or rebuked for this. Indeed, God seemed to share to the full the reaction of his friend. For God said to him, 'Your wife shall bear you a son, and you shall call his name "Laughter"' (Gen 17:19). What a friendship! Such was the strength of Abraham's relationship with God, so frequent and intimate was their communication with each other, that the New Testament calls him 'the friend of God' (Jas 2:23). In such a friendship Abraham knew what it was to laugh before the Lord. We know on the human level what a marvellous thing true friendship is, when you can be utterly at ease in another's company enjoying their companionship, sharing together confidences, expressing the emotion of the heart. This was the relationship that Abraham knew with God. The New Testament tells us (Gal 3:29) that belonging to Christ, we are Abraham's offspring —heirs according to the promise, children of the Spirit, children of laughter!

Sarah, Abraham's wife, on hearing the same message, also laughed (Gen 18:12). But it was a different kind of laughter to that of her husband. His was the laughter of surprise at the astounding ways of God. Hers was the laughter of cynicism. Listening at the tent door to the conversation of these desert travellers, her reaction seems to have been, 'Who do they think they're kidding?' But when she realized that it was the Lord who had spoken, she too believed with her husband that there is nothing too wonderful for the Lord. The whole project of two old people becoming parents is a demonstration of the foolishness of God that confounds the wisdom of men. So God enabled Sarah in her nineties to bear a son and, hugging her little baby, she could say: 'God has made laughter for me; everyone who hears will laugh with me' (Gen 21:6). Whether this refers to the actual laughter being heard or to the wondrous event that had taken place in Sarah's life is not clear. Perhaps both. We know that laughter in itself is infectious. You can laugh simply because others are laughing, but when laughter is created by the astounding doings of our God, that lifts it to a higher plane altogether.

How important it is for Christians today to emulate the example of Sarah, knowing God in such fellowship that, believing his astounding promises, we are made to laugh at his amazing deeds, and laughing in such a way that it causes others to laugh. This is a ministry conspicuous by its absence. It is high time for the sons of Abraham and the daughters of Sarah to bless the church and the world with God-given peals of laughter.

Mouths filled with laughter

When Israel sang in thanksgiving to God for their return from captivity, they recalled their emotions at the time of that great deliverance:

> When the Lord brought back the
> captive ones of Zion,
> We were like those who dream.
> Then our mouth was filled with laughter,

And our tongue with joyful shouting;
Then they said among the nations,
'The Lord has done great things for them.'
The Lord has done great things for us;
We are glad (Ps 126:1–3).

God filled their mouths with laughter and singing and it is not unusual in the experience of God's people today to know such laughter when the powerful operations of the Holy Spirit are evident; when he shows to the heart the astonishing deliverance wrought by Christ for undeserving captives; when he causes our chains to be broken and the heart to be set free from an evil conscience; when he actually conveys to our heart the love of God, shedding it abroad within us—sometimes our pent-up emotions find expression in gales of holy laughter. And it is because of what God has done—'The Lord has done great things for us; we are glad.'

A friend of mine was conducting a seminar on worship in South Africa. They had hired a conference room in a hotel for this and in the midst of their worship, contemplating and adoring the greatness of God and his mighty acts, unexpectedly and suddenly the whole company began to laugh and were soon convulsed in laughter. Laughter because of the greatness of God—of what he had done and what he would do. Suddenly they were aware of the hotel proprietor and his wife standing among them, surveying the scene. One of the ladies present went up to the wife only to discover that she was crying. This Christian girl explained to the wife that the people were laughing because they were so happy in God and both this woman and her husband were led to the Lord that afternoon. The laughter of God had brought tears to their eyes and through the conviction of the Spirit they were brought to trust in the Lord Jesus Christ.

14

Cultivating a Merry Heart

The title of this chapter comes from the Authorized Version of Proverbs 17:22—'A merry heart
doeth good like a medicine.' In other words it is
like a tonic both to yourself and indeed for others.
C. H. Spurgeon launched two evangelists into
their ministries, W. Y. Fullerton and Manton
Smith. Spurgeon said of the latter that to be with
him was as good as taking a fortnight's holiday. It
could be said of some people that to be with them
makes you feel that you *need* a fortnight's holiday.
We are poor advertisements for the God of joy if
we are gloomy and morose, if we allow circumstances to suffocate our joy. We need in this sickly
age Christian men and women who bring joy and
are a joy to others so that people feel benefited
and blessed in our company and give the glory to
God.

We can have a cheerful heart whatever our
temperament. One fact of life is very clear—that
there is great variety in the make-up of human

personalities. We all differ physically with various characteristics that mark us as the people we are, and this is no less true in regard to our personalities and temperaments. Some are extrovert and outgoing, happy-go-lucky and relaxed people: others are very much introverted, having a natural tendency, it seems, to look on the gloomy side of life—to be, in some cases, morbid. In other words there are by nature some people who are more cheerful than others and some who have a natural tendency to look on the gloomy side of life. There are the optimists and the pessimists.

It is important, I feel, that we recognize the fact of differences in our temperament. But, having stated that, I hasten to add that just as we should overwhelmingly conquer in all our circumstances, whatever they may be, so we must control our temperament and overwhelmingly conquer in that realm, whatever our temperament may be. So if a man is extrovert and optimistic and easy-going, he has to be on his guard against particular dangers—the danger of levity and flippancy and perhaps even unreality. Life is not one big joke, even though it can be very humorous, and unless my optimism finds its foundation in the written word of God, I am just building castles in the air. They are mere fiction.

Those who take a more dim view of life and tend to dejection of spirit must hear the word of God and hear it mixed with faith. Jesus says 'take courage: I have overcome the world' (Jn 16:33). Therefore do not give in to your temperament or yield to the temptation of saying, 'Well, I was born this way and can't do anything about it.' No, whatever our temperament we can overwhelmingly conquer. Dr Lloyd-Jones in his exposition of Romans 5 very vividly illustrates what I am trying to say. He speaks of going to hear a man preach on one occasion. He was a very godly man, earnest and a lover of the word of God, but one who had this disposition to look on the sadder side of life. On this particular day he chose to preach on 'The rainbow in the cloud' after the flood. Dr Lloyd-Jones records that he dealt with the reality of the cloud and its thickness and blackness and was so taken up with the cloud that they heard little or nothing about the rainbow. That, of course, is the tragedy of people who have that temperamental weakness. They see nothing but clouds.

> He was so afraid that we might go out with a carnal joy that he concealed the rainbow and magnified the cloud! That is not Scripture, that is not the balance of Scripture, that is not the proportion of faith. God's Word talks about the Rainbow and Cloud, and we must not try to be wiser than the Scriptures.[18]

I suppose it would be true to say that most of us alternate between these two extremes. Sometimes we are bright and happy and on other occasions we are sad and despondent. We oscillate between the peaks of spiritual blessing and the troughs of gloom and despondency. It is very important, therefore, that in the ups and downs of life we do not let our temperament or our moods govern us but, with our redeemed spirits, we learn through the power of the Spirit of God to govern our temperament. It is not without significance to me that both Luther and Spurgeon, men who could be ever so cheery and full of good humour, had to fight quite a fight of faith against intense attacks of depression. All of us, from time to time, fall into what Bunyan calls the Slough of Despond. What we have to realize is that we do not belong there and there is help from God to get us out.

During my time in India, I once was travelling on the public bus, which is a very hazardous venture anyway in India. The bus stopped and I alighted and had not noticed until it was too late that the bus had pulled up straight alongside the edge of the road. I stepped from the bus straight into a ditch, flat on my face. I lost my spectacles, I broke a tooth and I bruised my nose which was streaming with blood. I emerged, covered with dust and mud. But the great thing is—I emerged! And I did so pretty quickly for a ditch is not my natural habitat! We must take the same attitude and action when we fall into the Slough of Despond. It is not natural for us as Christians to stay there. We must do what the psalmist did. We must take ourselves in hand and even be severe with our own souls, questioning and saying, 'Why are you in despair, O my soul? And why have you become disturbed within me?' (Ps 42:5). Why? You have no valid reason for being blue and in the doldrums and certainly not for being in despair. Notice how the psalmist goes on to answer his own questions. He tells himself: 'Hope in God . . .' He brings God in on the scene and when God comes on the scene there is hope, no matter how dark and gloomy things may be. How can we be downcast? Our God lives. Our God loves. Our God saves. Our God has pledged his eternal convenant love to us and has assured us again and again that he will never leave us or forsake us. This is how we must take ourselves in hand whenever we are downcast. Then, like the psalmist, we shall 'yet praise Him, the help of [our] countenance, and [our] God' (Ps 42:11).

Many, I think, are depressed because they cannot throw off a sense of guilt. Some mistakenly believe that it is a sign of spiritual health to be introspective, constantly looking within, spying out their own weaknesses and failures, constantly telling themselves and God what miserable sinners they are. That, in my view, is a certain recipe for deep depression and may well have its root in unbelief that fails to take hold of the word of Christ 'Take courage . . . your sins are forgiven' (Mt 9:2). Some may say, 'Is it not the Holy Spirit who shows us our sins?' Yes, but he does it so that we may confess them and be cleansed from them so that, as Hudson Taylor reminds us, we can keep short accounts with God.

But let us recognize that the devil delights in accusing us. He has a vested interest in tormenting us with the memory of past sins. If he can he will shut us up into despair. This the Holy Spirit never does. He always reveals our sin in order to lead us to sin's only remedy—the blood of Jesus Christ that cleanses us from all sin. Let us not be ignorant of Satan's devices. John Bunyan was a wise pastor of souls. He tells us how Giant Despair was beheaded by Mr Great Heart. The Giant had been the cause of innumerable troubles and problems for the pilgrims whom he had taken captive and shut up in the prison of Doubting Castle. Mr Great Heart brought them the news of the Giant's defeat and showed them the evidence in displaying his severed head:

> Now, when Feeble-mind and Ready-to-halt saw that it was the head of Giant Despair indeed, they were very jocund and merry. Now Christiana, if need was, could play upon the viol, and her daughter Mercy upon the lute: so since they were so merry disposed, she played them a lesson, and Ready-to-halt would dance. So he took Despondency's daughter, Much-afraid, by the hand, and to dancing they went in the road. True, he could not dance without one crutch in his hand, but, I promise you, he footed it well: also the girl was to be commended, for she answered the music handsomely.[19]

Since Jesus has died and risen, sin and despair are defeated for ever. Have nothing to do with them. Refuse the lies of Satan. Believe the word of Christ. Cheer up! You, too, can join with the dancing in the road.

Our despondency is not always the work of the devil. Sometimes he gets blamed for that which can be attributed to other causes. Your despondency may be due to your indigestion! Are you in good shape physically? Are you in good shape mentally? Do you know what it is to relax? The string held taut is in danger of snapping. We all need recreation. We must not think that to do the work of God we always have to be engaging in what is known as 'Christ activities'. No, the work of God will not be brought to a halt because you have a day off. The kingdom of God will not collapse because you take a vacation. Look at the Lord Jesus with his disciples. Right in the midst of the crowds in all their need, with a very successful mission going on among them, Jesus said to the disciples, 'Come with me by yourselves to a quiet place and get some rest' (Mk 6:31, NIV). I wonder how they spent that time of recreation? This much is clear—that Jesus could see that it was needful. Don't overlook it. Be ready to relax and then come back refreshed into the work that God has given you to do.

If you would cultivate a merry heart, don't be a moaner. My wife and I were very amused on holiday in Spain when looking at the various menus displayed by the many restaurants that are to be seen advertising English breakfasts. One particular restaurant, added to the usual delights of eggs and bacon, also had toast and 'murmurlade'. I remarked to my wife that many people start the day with toast and 'murmurlade', and murmuring is something which comes in for condemnation in the word of God. It was a blot upon the life of the Israelites—they murmured in their tents (Deut 1:27). Paul in 1 Corinthians 10, enumerates the four major causes of Israel's failure in the wilderness. First, he highlights idolatry (v. 7) then immorality (v. 8), then testing the Lord (v.9) and finally, grumbling (v. 10). I wonder how many of us would put grumbling on a level with immorality and idolatry? But these things are brought together in the word of God and Paul bids us to do *all* things without grumbling. Instead of grumbling, try praising. 'In everything give thanks, for this is the will of God in Christ Jesus concerning you.'

The merry heart is a contented heart. Be content with such things as you have. Don't covet other people's possessions or gifts. Don't envy others. Don't seek to be what God never intended you to be. Rest in his sovereign assignments. He created you and redeemed you that you might, as a personality in your own right, reflect the glory of his beloved Son. Be content with that high destiny. Glory in God for that—that you are unique. Every human being is a unique creature and God can show his glory as Creator and Redeemer through you.

If you would be a tonic to others with a merry heart, share the optimism of God. The future is as bright as the promises of God. Well, let us be people who really build their lives upon the certainties of God's word. I like to stabilize my life on the 'shalls' of God's written word. So when temptation comes your way and it is strong and subtle, remember the 'shall' of God—'sin *shall not* have dominion over you' (Rom 6:14, RV). When in the cause of Christ on earth the church seems to be under assault from many quarters, remember the words of the Lord Jesus—'the gates of Hades *shall not* prevail against' the church which he is building (Mt 16:18, RV). And when, in your own work for God, you go through trying and testing times and the people are not turning to Christ in the measure you had hoped or prayed for, then believe the word that of the increase of Christ's kingdom '*there shall* be no end' (Lk 1:33, RV). And when this fallen world seems as if it is going from bad to worse and cruelty and lust are rife everywhere and the ungodly seem to be triumphing, remember what God has said—that 'the earth *shall be* filled with the knowledge of the glory of the Lord, as the waters cover the sea' (Hab 2:14, RV). I cannot think of any more sure method of maintaining a merry heart than simply founding and establishing one's life upon the sure promises of God.

Maintain a sense of humour. God made us with a sense of humour and he made us in his own image and he made us for his glory. Now the devil will seek to twist and pervert everything that God has made. Whereas God created all things—our abilities, our appetites—to be used for his honour and glory, the devil will tempt us and seek to get us to use these God-given abilities for dishonour. Many people have been troubled by what Paul says in Ephesians 5:4. Here he makes reference to 'filthiness and silly talk or coarse jesting which are not fitting'. People in reading that have said 'Is it wrong to joke or even to have fun?' Well, a glance at the context will soon give us the answer. Paul speaks first of all about misusing our bodies in immorality or impurity or greed, and he is dealing there with what we *do*. In verse 4 he comes to speak of what we *say* and he says filthiness or obscenity in our talk, even though it is under the guise of a joke, is not fitting. And just as we are to glorify God in our bodies, so we are to glorify God in our speech. Although the devil can get hold of joking and jesting, humour can be used for the glory of God—that is why God gave it to us—for we know it can save many a situation that is tense and perhaps embarrassing and is best passed off by a good hearty laugh. I recall reading how on one occasion C. H. Spurgeon answered his front door to be confronted by a man who was raving mad. He was brandishing a knife in his hand. Spurgeon said, 'What is it that you want?' He answered, 'I am looking for Spurgeon. I'm going to slit his throat from ear to ear!' With what seems to me to be a superb word of wisdom, Spurgeon calmly replied, 'Wouldn't that make a mess on the carpet?' 'Oh yes,' said the man. 'I never thought of that,' and turned round and went off on his way. Spurgeon never saw him again.

We know that humour can be an effective tool in teaching and preaching because, through humour, you can hammer home some deeply important and serious truths. In *George Whitefield: The Great Awakening* John Pollock recounts that wonderful story of when Whitefield first preached to the miners at Kingswood near Bristol, when the word of God went out with such a living impact on their hearts that it caused the tears to course down their cheeks, washing away the grime from their faces and making channels of white upon them. Many a time I have read the account and indeed used it as an illustration of what happens in times of revival, but it was Pollock's book that revealed to me that Whitefield began his address by telling a story which made the miners laugh. We read that they had never before 'heard a parson who had cracked a joke in a sermon'![20]

We may learn from this that humorous words are not necessarily idle words; humour can be harnessed to do the work of the Lord.

In considering the words of Scripture, 'All that

is within me . . .' (Ps 103:1) Spurgeon had this to say:

> . . . then let it be all. Some of us have a vein of humour, and though we try to keep it under constraint it will peep out. What then? Why, let it bear the Lord's yoke. This faculty is not necessarily common or unclean: let us make it a hewer of wood and drawer of water for the Lord.[21]

Jesus said, 'The good man out of the good treasure of his heart brings forth what is good . . . for his mouth speaks from that which fills his heart' (Lk 6:45). A heart filled with joy will minister joy to others.

A merry heart is not only a medicine, but a continual feast (Prov 15:15) that will provide an ample and enjoyable meal for many. Let us seek by the grace of Christ to spread a table in the wilderness for the hungry and sad, as we share the joy of the Lord with a merry heart.

15

Living Happily Ever After

The title of this chapter is taken from the story of Cinderella. You will remember that her prince had come, claimed her for his bride and changed all her future prospects. No more would she be the skivvy in the kitchen, no more cleaning the hearth, no more running about waiting on her ugly sisters; life promised to be one long ball—they lived happily ever after. We love a story to conclude in that way but it only happens in the realm of fiction; real life is not like that.

From what you have read concerning joy I hope it has become clear that the word of God is rooted in realism. It deals not with fiction but with facts. Nowhere does the Christian message of salvation and joy include a life insurance policy that guarantees freedom from life's troubles and pressures. We have seen that life is not all plain sailing; at times we travel through rough seas and stormy skies. But we have also seen that whatever our lot in life we can rejoice evermore in the Lord's presence, for his sure promise is that he will never leave us or forsake us—so we can rejoice in the Lord always. 'Always' means today and tomorrow, it means now and evermore. In that sense we can live happily ever after.

The reigning Lord

We have joy now in our reigning Lord. We can find ample and eternal reasons for rejoicing when we focus our faith upon the enthroned Christ. All authority is given to him in heaven and on earth, and this fact alone has set all heaven aglow with joy. He reigns, why should we ever be downcast? He has complete sovereignty over everything. Some will point to the world in which we live with its cruelty, violence, lust and consequent sorrows everywhere in evidence and they will ask how we can be joyful at such a time. These valid questions receive a complete answer in the word of God.

Habakkuk lived in such a time with the Chaldean army about to ravage the land and the ungodly seeming to triumph. It was a terrible time to live and the prophet could not understand the baffling chain of events that had transpired. So he took to his watch-tower and learning of God's ultimate purpose he soon came through to a glorious song of joy: 'Though the fig tree should not blossom, and there be no fruit on the vines, though the yield of the olive should fail, and the fields produce no food . . . yet I will exult in the Lord, I will rejoice in the God of my salvation' (Hab 3:17–18). His joy was not dependent on anything in his circumstances but in God himself.

We can rejoice always. Although circumstances may be hard and difficult to understand at times, the fact remains that God rules and overrules in all things. There is no despondency in heaven, there they see that the Lord our God the almighty reigns. They show us that the only appropriate response to this glorious fact is to rejoice and be glad and give the glory to him. This ensures our joy for all time and for all eternity.

As long as God reigns we can rejoice, and since he reigns for evermore we can rejoice evermore whatever tomorrow may bring—even when to-morrow may be the day of our death. For this is one day that will come for each one of us. We live in a time when men and women shy away from the thought of facing death but the indisputable fact is that sooner or later we shall all leave this world. Many of us are like the little child who prayed, 'Dear God, what is it like to die? I don't want to do it—I only want to know what it's like.' But is there any joy to be found in death? The New Testament has no doubt about this; it proclaims that Jesus by his death and resurrection has brought life and immortality to light by abolishing death. He has robbed death of its sting and the grave of its victory. Death retains the appearance of terror like a lion ready to devour but it is a lion with its teeth and talons drawn. Just as a mere painting of a fire cannot warm or consume, death —for every believer—has been divested of its power. It has been robbed of its sting and deprived of its victory. For the believer there is nothing to fear in death, rather we are assured that there is positive advantage. Paul tells us that 'to die is gain' (Phil 1:21). Many live in the hope of gain when someone else dies but the believer in Christ gains when he himself dies; he departs this world to be with Christ which is very much better. The believer enters the immediate presence of Christ, satisfied to awake in his likeness. In that eternal world of joy there is no more night, no more pain, no more tears and best of all, no more sin. There, joy knows no bounds—'"Blessed [or happy] are the dead who die in the Lord from now on!" "Yes," says the Spirit, "that they may rest from their labors, for their deeds follow with them"' (Rev 14:13). Thomas Watson expresses it beautifully when he says, 'In heaven there shall be joy and nothing but joy. Heaven is set out or explained by that phrase "Enter thou into the joy of the Lord". Here joy enters into us, there we enter into joy. The joys we have here are from heaven, the joys we shall have with Christ are without measure, and without mixture.'[22]

It is possible that some of us will not die physically at all, for there is a happy hope set before us in the appearing of the glory of our great God and Saviour, Jesus Christ. This same Jesus born of the Virgin Mary, anointed with the Spirit, rejected by men, crucified in weakness and raised in power, now enthroned in glory, will return to earth again. The event is absolutely sure, only the time is unknown. With glory and power, the Lord Jesus who ascended to heaven in the clouds will come again in like manner. The whole church of Christ will be caught up to meet the Lord in the air. That momentous event will bring us into an experience of unparalleled joy. If we rejoice now with 'joy unspeakable and full of glory', though we have never seen him, what raptures of joy await us when we actually look upon him?

We shall be like him

For we shall be like him and we shall be changed. Then our redemption will be complete. It is complete now in the sense that Christ has secured it for us but experientially we have only received it in part. We have redemption through his blood, even the forgiveness of our sins. We have received the down payment in the person of the Holy Spirit and he is the guarantee that the full amount will be given at the coming again of Christ. We shall know in our bodies the redemptive power of the Lord Jesus, for when he appears 'he will transform the body of our humble state into conformity with the body of His glory, by the exertion of the power that He has even to subject all things to Himself' (Phil 3:21).

Paul spells out what this means in 1 Corinthians 15:37–49, where he likens the burying of our bodies to a seed being sown in the ground. It is a most instructive illustration. When walking through a garden and your eyes feast upon the glory of a bed of petunias in their vivid colours or perhaps looking across the landscape you see the majesty and symmetry of a full-grown horse chestnut tree, the wonder of such a sight is increased when you remember that each grew from seeds. Each, according to their kind, were enclosed in the capsule of a seed, buried in the soil, nourished by the sun and rain and so realized their full potential. There is a relationship between what is sown and what grows from it; for you won't get a horse chestnut tree from a packet of petunia seeds. However the tree or the flower doesn't seem to bear much resemblance to the seed that was sown.

Paul argues that there is a relationship between the physical body we have now and the spiritual body that awaits us at the resurrection, but the glory of that spiritual body will outstrip the glory of our present bodies just as the full-grown tree, resplendent in foliage and flower, bears no comparison with the seed that was sown.

Paul says this will be the case with the resurrection of the dead. What is sown as a perishable body, is to be raised an imperishable body. It is sown in dishonour, it is raised in glory. It is sown in weakness, it is raised in power. It is sown a natural body, it is raised a spiritual body. Stephen Travis has said,

> The resurrected body of Jesus is the model for the resurrection of his followers. After Jesus rose from the dead he was no mere ghostly figure nor was he simply a physical body returned to life, his body was transformed suitable to life in a new and glorious environment. It was different yet still the same Jesus and so it shall be with us. Paul says we shall have spiritual bodies, personalities suited to a spiritual environment. We shall be no mere shadows of our former selves nor shall we be physical copies of our former selves—we shall be transformed for the life of heaven.[23]

I think we can afford ourselves the joy of anticipation of such a time when our bodies will be adapted to praise and serve our God for ever; no longer hampered by physical weakness or restricted by any kind of limitation our spiritual bodies will enable us to reach our full potential in our spiritual service. It will be an added joy, too, to see others of the household of faith who were enduring physical pain and limitation here on earth now set free for ever. No longer shall we hear the sad lament 'the spirit is willing but the flesh is weak'. When the last trumpet shall sound 'the dead will be raised imperishable, and we shall be changed' (1 Cor 15:52). There will be no more arthritis, no more multiple sclerosis, no more ageing and infirmity; disease and deformity will be vanished. Christ our Lord will do it by the power he has to subject everything to himself. What joy this very prospect should afford us now and what greater joy will be ours when we actually realize these things.

Our highest joy will be for the Lord himself. In that day he will be glorified and marvelled about by all who have believed. We shall see him in his glory. I wonder if you've ever tried to imagine what a person looks like having never met them before? You've heard about them, you've listened to descriptions of them from others and in your mind you begin to conjure up a picture of what they might look like. When you actually meet they are totally different to what you imagined them to be and frequently fail to live up to your expectations. I think that when at last we see Christ in all his glory, our highest expectations of him will be eclipsed as we look upon his excelling glory. We have our own ideas, we have intimations in his word, we have impressions and glimpses that quickly fade for we only see 'through a glass darkly' but then we shall see face to face. Now we only know in part but then we shall know fully just as we are fully known. We shall see him in his glory attended and adored by angels, we shall see him as the destined heir of all things, having gathered up all things under him. We shall see him acknowledged by all, even his enemies falling at his feet. We shall see him reigning supreme over all. In such an hour our testimony will be like that of the Queen of Sheba who came to see the wealth and hear the wisdom of Solomon. When she saw the glory of Solomon's kingdom she said, 'The half was not told me. You exceed in wisdom and prosperity the report which I heard. How blessed are your men, how blessed are these your servants who stand before you continually' (1 Kings 10:7–8).

> O the joy to see Thee reigning,
>   Thee, our own beloved Lord,
> Every tongue Thy name confessing,
> Worship, honour, glory, blessing
>   Brought to Thee with one accord;
> Thee our Master and our Friend,
>   Vindicated and enthroned,
> Unto earth's remotest end,
>   Glorified, adored and owned.
>
> *F. R. Havergal*

Notes

1. Andrew Bonar, *Memoir and Remains of Robert Murray M'Cheyne* (Oliphant Anderson and Farrier, 1892), p.23.
2. A. P. Fitt, *D. L. Moody* (Moody Press), p.81.
3. B. F. Westcott, *The Epistle to the Hebrews* (Macmillan, 1892), p.27.
4. John Bunyan, *Pilgrim's Progress* (Religious Tract Society) pp.45–46.
5. C. H. Spurgeon, *Autobiography Vol. 2: The Full Harvest 1860–1892* (Banner of Truth, 1973), p.426.
6. J. I. Packer, *Keep in Step with the Spirit* (IVP, 1984), pp.112–113.
7. Michelle Guinness, *Child of the Covenant* (Hodder & Stoughton, 1984), p.117.
8. F. D. Bruner, *A Theology of the Holy Spirit,* (Hodder & Stoughton, 1971), p.133.
9. Robert Lacey, *Majesty* (Hutchinson), p.265.
10. Packer, *Keep in Step with the Spirit*, p.253.
11. C. H. Spurgeon, *The Treasury of David*

(Passmore and Alabaster, 1898), vol. 7 p.464.
12. G. A. Williamson (ed). *Fox's Book of Martyrs* (Secker and Warburg), p.237.
13. John Wimber, *Power Evangelism* (Hodder & Stoughton, 1985), p.98.
14. Winston S. Churchill, *The Second World War, Vol. 1: The Gathering Storm* (Cassel, 1948), p.526.
15. A. T. Pierson, quoted in Leslie Flynn, *Serve the Lord with Gladness* (1971).
16. Charles Stanford, *Wit and Humour of Life* (Elliot Stock).
17. Ibid.
18. Martyn Lloyd-Jones, *Romans An Exposition of Chapter 5: Assurance* (Banner of Truth, 1971), p.166.
19. Bunyan, *Pilgrim's Progress*, p.292.
20. John Pollock, *George Whitefield and the Great Awakening* (Lion, 1982), p.83.
21. C. H. Spurgeon, *The Metropolitan Tabernacle Pulpit, vol. 18* (Banner of Truth), p.607.
22. Thomas Watson, *Body of Divinity* (Banner of Truth, 1970), p.272.
23. Stephen Travis, *The Jesus Hope* (IVP, 1980), p.73.